Time Detectives
Clues from our Past

written by

Donalda Badone

Annick Press Ltd.
Toronto, Canada

© 1992 Donalda Badone (text)

Design by Brian Bean

Cover illustration by Brian Bean

Text illustrations by Joe Morse; 12, 13, 20, 42, 52, 53, 63, 74, 85, 98, 99, 100. Lorraine Tuson; 9, 19, 29, 39, 49, 61, 73, 83, 89, 97. Leon Zernitsky; 16, 17, 26, 27, 36, 37, 45–47, 57, 58, 69–71, 80, 81, 87, 94, 95, 102, 103, 105.

Annick Press Ltd.

Annick Press gratefully acknowledges the support of the Canada Council and the Ontario Arts Council.

Canadian Cataloguing in Publication Data

Badone, Donalda
    Time detectives : clues from our past

ISBN 1-55037-240-8

I. Archaeology – Study and teaching (Elementary) –
Canada. I. Title.

CC171.B33 1992   j971′.007   C92-094768-9

The text for this book has been set in Garamond and Univers by Attic Typesetting.

Distributed in Canada and the USA by:
Firefly Books Ltd.
250 Sparks Avenue
Willowdale, Ontario M2H 2S4

∞ Printed on acid-free paper.

Printed and bound in Canada by
D.W. Friesen and Sons, Altona, Manitoba.

For Amy, and the next generation

Contents

When you see a small number like this [1] after a quotation, look in this section. It will tell you where the information in the quotation came from.

Archaeology Uncovers Canada's Hidden Past

Why do archaeologists dig?

All across Canada the mysteries are being solved. Archaeologists are reading the hidden history of our past, not in the pages of a book, but in the layers of an excavation. Sometimes, like detectives, they are thrilled by a dramatic breakthrough; more often, discoveries come only after slow and careful investigation. Only a few of the thousands of sites across Canada are reported here.

Could a dig solve a mystery where you live?

It happened to one young person.

Flash

The Globe and Mail, May 1989

Somewhere in Metro Toronto today, Dr. Mima Kapches is beginning an archaeological dig.

While other Canadian archaeologists are screening the sands of the Nile River, digging into ancient river beds in Iraq, resisting the sun's hot rays in the Chihuahua desert in Mexico looking for dinosaurs or scraping the jungle floor in Belize, Dr. Kapches is "digging" in a family's backyard.

Why? She is curious about Toronto's prehistoric residents.

For several years, Dr. Kapches has been engineering digs around Metro and tracing the last mammoths, giant relatives of today's elephant, that pastured in the area near Yonge and Bloor streets centuries ago.

But this is the first time Dr. Kapches, an assistant curator at the Royal Ontario Museum, has moved optimis-

Archaeological Resource Centre,
Toronto Board of Education

tically into someone's backyard.

Scientifically, Dr. Kapches says, she is going out to excavate a site. . . .

She found [it] through a child's curiosity two years ago. 'I was lecturing at a school and a student showed me an artifact that had been found in his backyard. We were given permission for a test that October.'

Test digs unearthed a campsite . . . [which] . . . may be from the late Archaic or early Woodland periods. 'It's really exciting', she said.

It's happening right across Canada!

From Labrador in the east to Vancouver in the west and from the Niagara Peninsula to Baffin Island archaeologists are at work.

Why is it important—why do archaeologists dig?

They would answer that it tells us about people who lived long ago—the Woodland First Nation people around Toronto, the Norse in Newfoundland. If we didn't carefully excavate where they left their traces, we wouldn't know anything about them. They didn't write books to tell us about their lives. It's only by investigating the things they left behind that the time detectives can find out about the way they lived. That's what archaeologists do.

But doesn't everyone know that archaeology is digging up buried treasure! Finding mummies in Egypt! Breaking into old tombs for jewels and gold!

All these exciting things do sometimes happen—but only by chance. The real work of archaeology is the study of people through their physical remains, the things they used and left behind. They may never have been valuable. Most are everyday items.

Real discoveries result from hands-on experience at the Archaeological Resource Centre, Toronto Board of Education.

What did the archaeologists find at L'Anse aux Meadows at the northern tip of Newfoundland? The clues they found were so important to the whole world that, in 1978, it became the first site to be placed on Unesco's World Heritage List.

To find out more about those clues, let's go back with the time detectives to a summer nearly a thousand years ago.

L'Anse aux Meadows

Newfoundland

A surfacing whale might have spouted with astonishment at something it had never seen before. In front of it were wooden ships, their high proud prows cresting the waves. Along the side of one, a row of brown-clad figures pointed and shouted excitedly. Olaf pushed in front, rubbing sleepy eyes. He had just left the shelter that covered people, animals and cargo together. It was dark and smelly there, but warm. The icy wind off the floating bergs pierced his leather jacket. Brawny arms made a place for the youngest crew member to see.

"What is it?"

"Land, land!" shouted the men.

"See, grass for the cows! A stream for drinking water!"

The green line of the shore grew nearer. Olaf rubbed his eyes again. Was this lonely, silent place to be the new settlement? Was this the rich and fertile land he had heard so much about?

The sagas of the Vikings are tales of adventure and exploration. From Norway, seafaring heroes had sailed to Greenland, then on to Iceland. It was Bjarni Herjolfsun who, on a voyage from Iceland to Greenland, became lost in fog and winds and sighted a strange land. But it was Leif Eiriksson, Leif the Lucky, who the sagas say "bought Bjarni's ship from him and engaged a crew" to see for himself the new found land and bring back its treasures. He made landfall at "a place where a river flowed out of a lake." The saga also says "There were fields of wheat grown wild and there were vines as well, and large trees....they decided to winter there, and built some large houses."[1] Leif called his new domain Vinland.

Then, for centuries, no traces of Norse occupation were found. Was Vinland part of North America? If so, where could it be?

In 1960 a cruising whale might have spotted another Norse adventurer. The story of Leif the Lucky and his discovery of a new world fascinated Helge Ingstad and his wife, Anne Stine, an archaeologist. They had searched the Atlantic coast looking for a bay that fitted the description of the Vinland of the sagas.

L'Anse aux Meadows was their last port of call. From the small fishing village a man came walking towards them. It was George Decker. He had lived in the isolated area all his life. When asked about old house sites, he said, "Yes, there is something like that over by Black Duck Brook." . . . Almost in his backyard, you might say.

They walked round the bay. No doubt about it, thought Ingstad, these are the remains of houses.

"Who were the people who lived here?" he asked Decker.

"No one knows. They were here before the fishermen came. . . . And my family were the first to settle here."

Ingstad says, "There was so much here at L'Anse aux Meadows that reminded me of what I had seen of the surroundings of the Norse farms in Greenland; the green fields, the rippling stream, the open country, the view of the sea. . . . Here [the Vikings] would have felt at home.

Opposite page above: The 1976 crew is happy with their progress in spite of cold and wet weather.

Below, archaeologist Birgitta Wallace checks the records of the day's excavation.

Parks Canada

Parks Canada

"But so far everything was uncertain; only digging could reveal to us the secrets in the ground."[2]

Now it was the turn of the archaeologist—the time detective—in this case, Anne Stine.

She and the other archaeologists who have worked on the site found no buried treasure, no jewels or gold, not even a skeleton. They did find examples of two types of clues to the past—features in the earth, and artifacts.

Features are marks or remains that tell of human activity. They may be holes in the ground or coloured stains left by fire or the rotting of wood. Of course, they cannot be moved. In the lonely Newfoundland cove Ingstad and Anne Stine saw bumps and ridges in the grass. Careful excavations of this area were undertaken by Anne Stine in the early years and later by Canadian Parks Services, first under Bengt Schonback and then under Birgitta Wallace. The features proved to be what was left of the walls of eight Norse buildings dating back to the eleventh century.

Other features were uncovered—a fireplace with a flat stone as a floor and a nearby pit containing charcoal, indicating fire, and probably used for cooking.

The style of the dwellings, with sod walls and roof covering a wood frame, was the same as that of houses in Greenland and Iceland at the same time.

Parks Canada

Replicas of some of the sod buildings at L'Anse aux Meadows let us see what life was like for Olaf and the other Norse settlers.

Below is a ringed bronze pin for fastening cloaks. Invented in Ireland, it was used by the Norse wherever they settled in the Celtic lands of Ireland and Scotland, and in Iceland.

Opposite page: Soapstone spindle whorls, like the one in the drawing, were commonly found during the Viking age throughout the entire Norse region.

The artifacts found inside the buildings were also clues to who the people were and what they were doing there. An artifact is an object that has been altered or used by human beings—it might be a coin or just a piece of rock formed into a tool.

In the ruins of the houses at L'Anse aux Meadows were small, useful items—a spindle whorl for spinning wool and a fragment of a bone needle. A more unusual find was a bronze ring-topped pin used to fasten a cloak. What did this collection tell the archaeologist-detectives?

Spindle whorls and needles were used by women. This was not only a voyage for the purpose of exploration. The leaders of the expedition must have brought their wives to the site, perhaps hoping to start a new settlement.

In all, the community consisted of three large houses with nearby workshops. It has been suggested that one of the rooms was used by the women for the production of clothing. Raw wool was fastened to a spindle, a notched stick weighted at the bottom with a spindle whorl like the one that was found at the site. The spindle was dropped and twisted to form yarn. In other Norse areas of the time an upright loom was used to weave the yarn into fabric for all the clothing worn by the people. One of the rooms might have been used for this purpose.

Evidence was found of a blacksmith's workshop and a furnace hut by the brook. One of the attached workshops was used by blacksmiths to make nails.

It was these working areas which did much to lead the archaeologists to believe this really was a Norse site. Most impressive was the simple smithy. Bog iron ore, found along the banks of the brook, was heated with charcoal in the furnace (a pit lined with clay and topped with stones). The iron produced was reheated and hammered out; then the smiths forged it and made the nails and rivets needed to repair the ships. Used, discarded iron rivets cut from the boats showed where they were repaired. Wood debris was found near one of the buildings — remains from a carpentry shop.

From all the archaeological evidence it was deduced that L'Anse aux Meadows was a settlement used by people from Greenland for exploring the continent of North America. It was occupied for only a few years.

Whether the little village was the Vinland of the sagas is open to question. Birgitta Wallace, the archaeologist who for many years directed the project, sees L'Anse aux Meadows as the *gateway* to Vinland.

From the settlement at the cove the Norse could venture forth to explore all around the Gulf of St. Lawrence. Travelling along the coastline down into New Brunswick and Nova Scotia the seafarers could have seen and gathered abundant wild fruit, including the grapes that gave their name, Vinland, to the area. Three butternuts, recovered from the fen, show how far south the explorers must have travelled, since butternut trees do not grow north of New Brunswick.

It would have needed a strong and fearless leader to organize and carry out these perilous expeditions. Leif the Lucky was such a man. By establishing his settlement at L'Anse aux Meadows he would have controlled the entrance to a rich and varied region.

Why then was it occupied for only a few years? Perhaps the native people living nearby overwhelmed the settlers. (The sagas tell of battles with someone the Norse called "skraelings".) Or it may have been that the voyage across the treacherous North Atlantic from Greenland was just too dangerous for such uncertain rewards.

What we know is that a small number of hardy and fearless Viking men and women came ashore at this lonely spot, pleased with the expanse of grass for their livestock, the brook of fresh water running down to the sea and the beach where they could haul up their boats for repair.

They left their mark for archaeologists to find, and record, the earliest known European habitation in the whole of the Americas.

The time detectives can't tell us what happened to Olaf. The sagas do say that one day in Vinland, Karlsefni's wife, Gudrid, gave birth to a son. Could he have been a little brother, the first European baby to be born in North America? Could he have been born in one of the houses at L'Anse aux Meadows?

Clues

Features are clues that archaeologists use as evidence that people have occupied a site. They must be studied where they are. They cannot be moved to a laboratory for examination.

At L'Anse aux Meadows archaeologists found the remains of walls. Layers of sod had been piled up on top of one another. The upper ones had worn away but the lower part had not yet completely disappeared. As the walls were uncovered, they became features to be plotted on the map of the site.

Parks Canada

This house, shown above as it was being excavated, and in the plan below, contains four rooms all in a row. Since the sod had to provide insulation, the walls were wide, up to two metres in places.

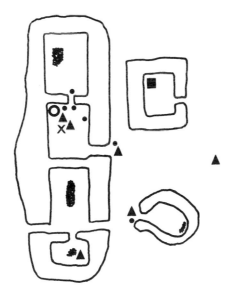

✳ hearth
◯ ringed pin
• iron nail/rivet
✕ bone artifact
■ roasted bog ore
▲ bone

Inside the buildings, careful scraping revealed stains in the soil. The lighter stains were made by wood which had rotted. This clue led our archaeologist-detectives to believe that the sod houses had had wooden supports. The darker stains were in the middle of the floor and contained charcoal — evidence of the fires used for cooking and heating.

Archaeologists also find artifacts.

An artifact is an object which has been used or altered by human action. It can be removed from the site for study and to be shown in a museum.

At L'Anse aux Meadows a spindle whorl, a needle and a cloak pin were found.

What did these discoveries reveal about the settlement? They tell us that since it was usually women who spun and knitted, it is likely that families lived at the site. They probably had animals with them — sheep for the wool to spin and turn into clothing. They evidently dressed in cloth in addition to the fur and skins worn by the native people.

The ringed pin was an especially good clue. It could be compared to other pins that were known to be used elsewhere by Norse people at that time to fasten their woollen cloaks.

In the workshops other artifacts were found — wood debris and slag from the smelting and working of iron, and boat nails and rivets. The inhabitants of the site knew how to work iron. They must have come from a place, and at a time, when that was commonly done. Since they used the iron to replace the rivets in their boats they must have been a seafaring people.

Adding together all the evidence from the features and the artifacts, the archaeologists inferred, or deduced, a whole picture of European life at L'Anse aux Meadows.

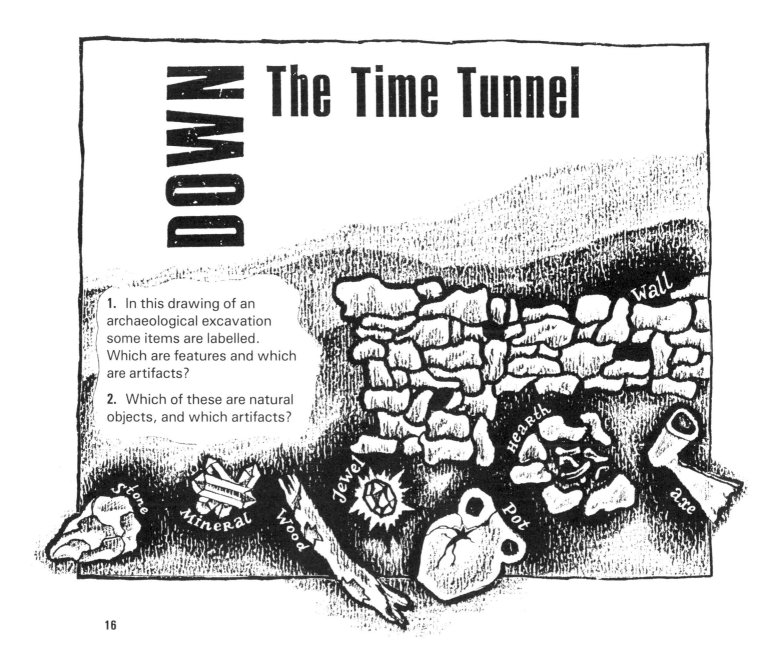

DOWN The Time Tunnel

1. In this drawing of an archaeological excavation some items are labelled. Which are features and which are artifacts?

2. Which of these are natural objects, and which artifacts?

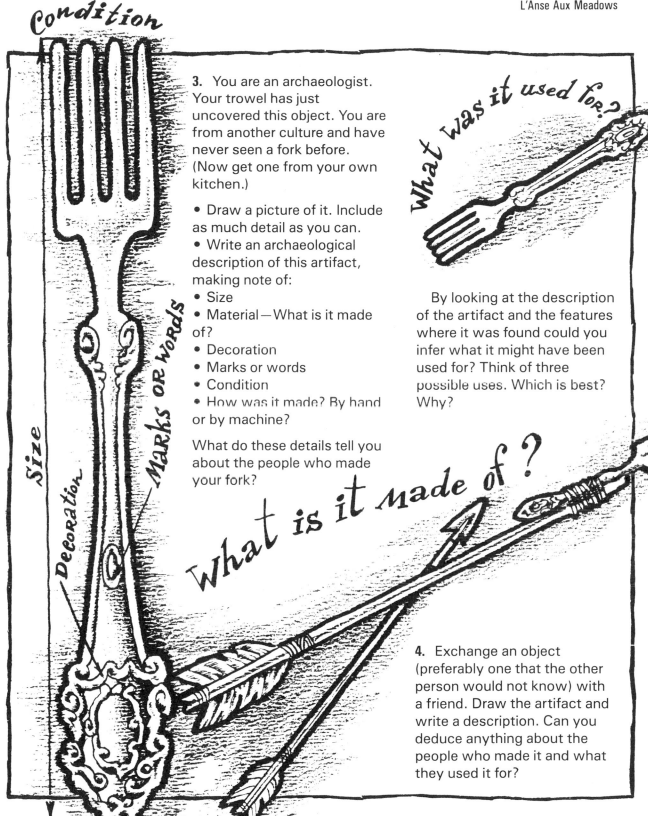

Condition

Size

Decoration

Marks or words

What was it used for?

What is it made of?

3. You are an archaeologist. Your trowel has just uncovered this object. You are from another culture and have never seen a fork before. (Now get one from your own kitchen.)

• Draw a picture of it. Include as much detail as you can.
• Write an archaeological description of this artifact, making note of:
• Size
• Material—What is it made of?
• Decoration
• Marks or words
• Condition
• How was it made? By hand or by machine?

What do these details tell you about the people who made your fork?

By looking at the description of the artifact and the features where it was found could you infer what it might have been used for? Think of three possible uses. Which is best? Why?

4. Exchange an object (preferably one that the other person would not know) with a friend. Draw the artifact and write a description. Can you deduce anything about the people who made it and what they used it for?

Louisbourg

Nova Scotia

A small girl and boy walk along the seafront towards the Porte Dauphine. A sentry calls out in French, "Qui va là?" They give their names.

"Ah, oui. I know that name. Passez, passez," says the soldier. "Go through!"

He recognizes their last name! Does he know that their ancestor once lived here, was challenged and passed through these same gates perhaps a hundred times? Have they been travelling not only in space, from France, but also back in time to the eighteenth century? Marie-Louise and Jean walk along the path toward the spires of the town, a path they have never travelled and yet know so well.

It seems like a fairytale that they should be returning to the place so familiar from Grandmère's stories. *Her* grandmother told of lying in bed and seeing a cannonball burst through the bedroom wall during the terrible siege. The mighty Fortress of Louisbourg looks just like it must have done in 1758 when the children's aieux (ancestors) had been sent back to France. They knew the town was in ruins at that time. They had come back across the ocean to see how it had risen again.

When Louisbourg was founded in 1713 on Cape Breton Island in Nova Scotia, it was the most magnificent place in North America. Travellers compared it to a French metropolis, looming strangely above the wild, uninhabited shore. "A strong and fabled city", it was said, "like some magic scene".[3]

Legend has it that so much money was spent on the Fortress of Louisbourg that King Louis XV expected to wake up one morning in Paris and see the towers rising out of the Atlantic.

In France medals were struck with the profile of the young king on one side and the words Ludovico-burgum Fundatum et Munitum MDCCXX (Louisbourg Founded and Fortified, 1720) on the reverse. Nearly 250 years later one of these was among the first artifacts dug up by archaeologists at the site.

The great fortress cost so much because almost nothing was made in Louisbourg; nearly all had to be brought in by ship. Stone and brick were imported from France. Lumber and flour came from New England. Vegetables and livestock were raised by the settlers in nearby Acadia. Coffee and sugar was brought by ship from the West Indies. Pottery and glass came from France, England, Italy, Germany, Spain and even China.

The only item Louisbourg had for export was fish. It was to protect the cod fishing fleet and provide a base for French trading interests in the "new" world that Louisbourg was built.

It lasted only 45 years.

During that time it was besieged, captured and given back to the French by British forces. In 1758 it was again overcome. To put an end to the threat it posed, the British Commander-in-Chief in North America was told by his prime minister "the Fortress, together with all the works, and Defences of the

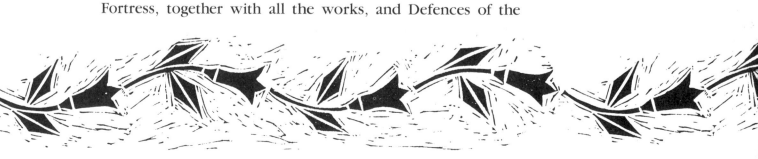

Harbour, [must] be most effectually and entirely demolished."

Barrel after barrel of gunpowder was placed in 45 specially dug holes in the ground and detonated at dawn. The fort was left in ruins, its stones plundered for use elsewhere. The inhabitants, including the ancestors of Marie-Louise and Jean, were sent back to France.

The surprising fact is that the site had only a few occupants for the next 200 years. William C. MacKinnon of Sydney, Nova Scotia, wrote:

I stand on a grassy plain—I see
Nothing around that recalls to me
That city, the queen of the western sea.
There the bay's glassy waters sleep—
Here graze amid grey ruins, sheep—
Her pomp is gone, her streets are lone,
Her ramparts are with grass o'ergrown. . . .[4]

At the turn of this century some restoration was done but it was not until the 1920s that people began to take a real interest in Louisbourg. Parts of the site were cleared and in 1928 it was established as a National Historical Park. In 1961 the government announced plans for a reconstruction of the fortress.

Parks Canada

Only the ruins of a few stone walls were left on the site of the mighty Fortress of Louisbourg when the restoration began in this century.

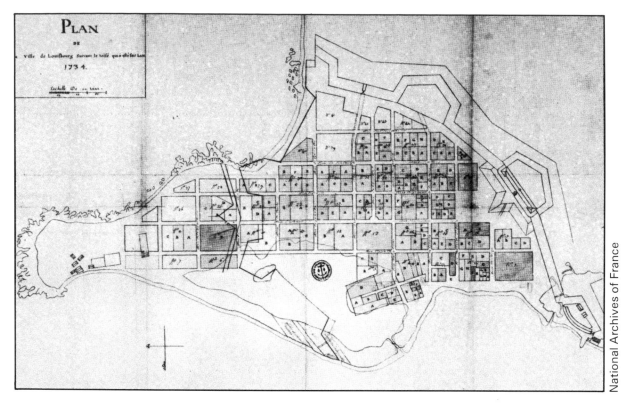

National Archives of France

Once more it was the turn of the time detectives, this time to uncover the secrets of Louisbourg—to reveal the original fortress so that its restoration would be authentic in every detail.

How did they know where to start digging? There were many good clues. On the ground, ruins of walls could still be seen. Local people had stories to tell of features and artifacts found. And, most fortunately, and most unusually, it was possible to go to France and find the 500 plans and hundreds of documents concerning the original construction.

Archaeologists and historians pooled their knowledge with engineers and architects. Today more than 50 eighteenth century buildings have been reconstructed and furnished to show how people lived and worked in Louisbourg. 1744 was chosen because that was the year when the fate of the fortress hung in the balance: war had been declared but Louisbourg had not yet been attacked.

Restoration archaeology has been called Humpty Dumpty archaeology—through team work, all the pieces are put back

A plan of Louisbourg, drawn in 1734, shows the bastions looking out, ready to defend the town from enemies approaching from the sea.

together again to provide a three-dimensional portrait of life at the time.

Because the site was so undisturbed, archaeologists at Louisbourg have one of the largest and most varied collections of eighteenth century artifacts. It is used by other institutions when they are restoring sites of the same period. It has been said that "as many as two million wood, iron, ceramic, glass and leather artifacts have been unearthed at Louisbourg."[5] This number has now been increased to five million.

Pottery for Louisbourg is made in much the same way it was in 18th century France. Reproduced from pieces recovered during the excavations, and researched historically, it is used in the restored houses and inns.

Costumed interpreters go about the daily business of Louisbourg just as they would have in 1744. The site is unusually rich in historical documents—church registers of baptisms, marriages and burials; records of legal transactions concerning property; sentences handed down by the courts; and lists of people and cargo arriving by ship.

Louis Badone

Parks Canada

Life in the 18th century is recreated to-day. At right, processing the cod that was the basis of Louisbourg's trade.

It would not be impossible for Marie-Louise and Jean, visiting from France, to see a reconstruction of the very same house their ancestors lived in.

From the bright street, they step into the shadowy kitchen. How strange to go back in time! Before them they see great-great-great Grandmère pouring batter for thin apple-filled Breton crepes (like pancakes), while great-great-great Grand-père mends his fishing net in the corner.

Clues

Very few archaeological sites are as well documented as Louisbourg. How do archaeologists find sites to dig where there are not such good clues?

An archaeological site is any place where there is evidence of human activity. It consists of features and artifacts. Like Louisbourg it may be a place where people lived for many years or it could be a fishing camp used only in the spring. People do not need to have lived on a site; they might gather there to bury their dead or paint pictures at a sacred rock. It could be a place where stone is quarried to make tools.

Some sites are found by chance—perhaps an artifact is turned up by a plough. Most are found by archaeologists making systematic surveys.

A crew walks the field looking for traces of human activity. If an artifact or the remains of a feature are spotted, a test pit may be dug to see whether further work will uncover the site the archaeologist's research has shown to be in the area.

Bob Burgar

First the archaeologist-detective will do research in libraries and archives. The lifestyle of the people tells the archaeologist what to look for. For example, if they had enemies, they would have needed to protect themselves, perhaps by building a shelter under a cliff. A village will need a source of food and water. The archaeologist looks at maps and aerial surveys and can see where sites are likely to be found.

When a general idea of where to look has been formed, a crew is gathered to walk over the ground looking for features and artifacts. A plan, or grid, is drawn up so that these clues can be located accurately. Sometimes they are marked with a red flag. Then, if the results look promising, the archaeologists will have one or more test pits dug.

When there is little to see on the ground, the archaeologist takes to the air. Many important sites have shown up in photographs taken from an airplane. Earth that has been disturbed by digging for a crop or for a building never quite returns to its original state. Aerial photography will pick up colour differences or ridges which are difficult to spot from the ground.

More advanced and expensive methods for detecting underground disturbances include TIMS—the thermal infrared multispectral scanner which detects the temperature and energy release of different materials. A straight line revealed through this tool might indicate, for instance, a buried stone wall.

The dig site is always chosen to answer a specific question. Perhaps the people involved in reconstruction need to know where a special activity was carried on. At Louisbourg, it might be to find the place where codfish were processed. At another site, an archaeologist may be called in because of threatened damage to the area by construction of a road or houses. A site may be in danger from natural causes, such as floods. Even if the site itself cannot be saved, the archaeologist gains knowledge from its excavation.

pegs

DOWN The Time Tunnel

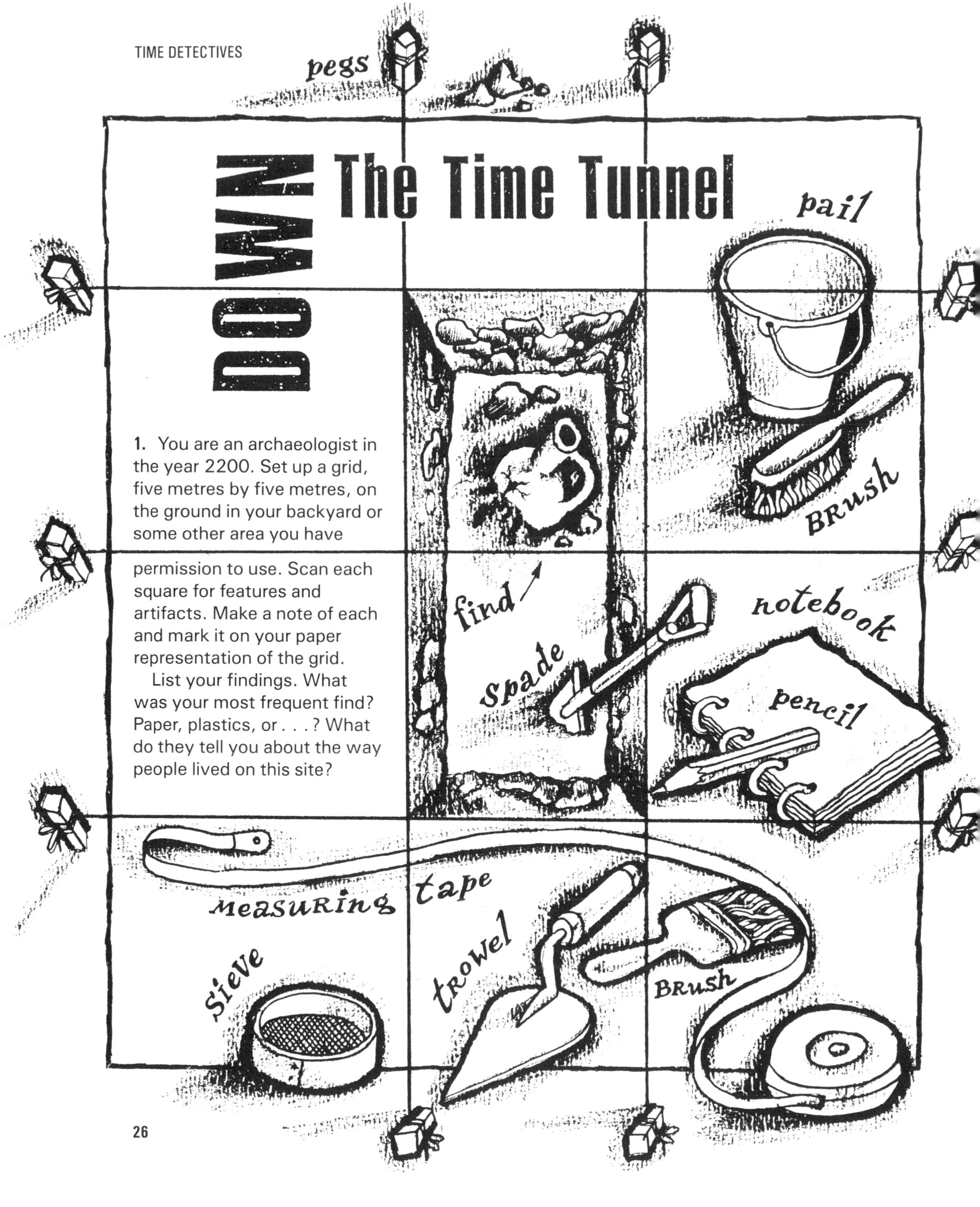

pail

BRush

find →

Spade

notebook

pencil

1. You are an archaeologist in the year 2200. Set up a grid, five metres by five metres, on the ground in your backyard or some other area you have permission to use. Scan each square for features and artifacts. Make a note of each and mark it on your paper representation of the grid.

List your findings. What was your most frequent find? Paper, plastics, or . . . ? What do they tell you about the way people lived on this site?

measuring tape

sieve

trowel

BRush

Mountains

Sea

River

Why did people decide to live where you do?

• Do you call it a city, town, village, farm or . . . ?

• What is the oldest thing here?

• Was there ever a battle here?

• Is there evidence of industries, trade, religious life as in Louisbourg?

• What do the different types of houses tell about the people who live in Louisbourg? What do they tell about the people where you live?

2. Why did people decide to live where you do? Archaeologists look for sites which provide shelter, food and water.

• Were any of these available when the first settlers came to your area?

Place Royale

Québec City

"Time for bed. Pick up your toys."

"Pleeaase. . . Only one more piece and my tower is finished! But where is it? It was in my hand a minute ago. Now it's gone!"

Sound familiar? No doubt it echoed through the centuries in Place Royale in Québec City. Among the toys and game pieces lost there over the years, many were later found by the archaeological-detectives in the house called la maison Paradis on rue Notre Dame. Along with other artifacts, 56 marbles, a doll's tea set, three wooden dominoes, two doll's heads and a doll's arm, rubber balls, plastic spectacles and a DC8 airplane have been recovered in recent excavations. The maison Paradis has a long history of children playing there!

Place Royale is where Champlain built his first habitation in 1608 when he came from France to trade in furs with the native people. Here was the beginning of the history of French-speaking people in North America.

In 1637 the Jesuit fathers were given a piece of land by the Governor to build a store house. Their goods were unloaded from boats coming up the St. Lawrence River and were held in their building on rue Notre Dame where the maison Paradis now stands. In 1683 they sold the property to Philippe Gauthier de Comporté, one of the founders of the Company of the North formed to trade in furs. He and his wife, Marie, had children; we know this because a document tells us a guardian was appointed for them when their father died in 1687.

Another family living on the property in the seventeenth and eighteenth centuries was that of Louise Douaire de Bondy. She was married twice, first to another fur trader and explorer, Pierre Allemand, and later to Nicolas Pinault, a merchant. Louise outlived both her husbands and remained in the same house for 58 years, until her death in 1746. We know she had at least one child, Marie-Thérèse Allemand, who is listed in an early census.

Oeuvres de Champlain

Louis Badone

Did the Gauthier children or Marie-Thérèse play with the oldest marbles found on the site?

In 1759 the buildings on it were burned in the siege of Quebec by the British. Joseph Paradis built a new house and store there in 1762.

After the British occupation there were a number of other owners and people who rented part of the building. In 1782 it was bought by William Laing, a draper, who imported and sold linens and clothing. He owned it for 29 years, until 1811. Perhaps he, too, raised a family in the part of the house that was not used for business. If so, the Laing children could have lost the pieces of the tea set which dates to that period.

Opposite page above: A drawing of Champlain's Habitation, 1608.

Opposite page below: The maison Paradis has stood on rue Notre-Dame for over two hundred years. It is now being restored to look as it did when it was first built.

At right, a painting by William Berczy shows the family of Mr. Woolsey, a wealthy Québec merchant. The children were well supplied with amusements.

National Gallery of Canada

A little later, another merchant family called Torrance became the owners of the maison Paradis. It remained in their possession for 81 years, from 1811 to 1892. In the early part of the nineteenth century Isabella and William Torrance were living there. They had five children—John, Henry, Isabella Amelia, Matilda and Sophia. Did one of them throw the head of a sister's doll down the latrine? It lay there for at least a century before archaeologists found it again.

By the late nineteenth and twentieth centuries the neighbourhood had become less grand. The interior of the maison

Paradis was divided into many flats and rented out to many tenants. Some must have had children who would have enjoyed playing in the courtyard in the rear of the property.

One of the tenants, Dr. John Henchey, had his medical office in the building, and in 1895 he complained about the noise the children made.

"The yard", he said, "is daily and constantly frequented by boys [who] scream, shriek and howl in such manner and create such disturbance as to seriously interfere with business."[6]

No doubt the boys lost a large number of the marbles found years later. Did they bounce their rubber balls off the stone walls of the courtyard and make Dr. Henchey's head ring?

For 300 years children have played on the property known as the maison Paradis. Perhaps to them the courtyard was a little paradise—a haven away from the crowded streets. Through the work of the archaeologists we know some of their games and toys.

You may be among the lucky ones who have visited Quebec City with your school or with relatives. If so, you will have seen the wonderful restoration of the streets around the Place Royale. They look now as they did during the French regime of the eighteenth century.

Reconstruction began in 1970. The work of archaeologists was different from that at Louisbourg. There the site was a grassy plain; here at Quebec a modern city had risen with roads and traffic, electricity lines, water and sewer pipes. Even now, visitors must watch out for machinery as the work goes on. The maison Paradis is one of the houses being restored today.

The artifacts found by the time detectives give life to the historical accounts of Place Royale. They permit the archaeologist to reconstruct human behaviour of this bygone era and answer questions about past activities. For example: what went on behind the trading counters and warehouses of the merchants? The large collection of playthings indicates a rich family life in which children must have been valued. The latest fashions in toys were imported to amuse them.

The collection also has more practical uses. In the whole of Place Royale 238 marbles were found. 117 of them were made

Rue Notre-Dame, below, leads down to Place Royale and the church which stands on the site of Champlain's Habitation. Lines on the pavement in the square at right mark the outline of the original fort.

Louis Badone

Louis Badone

of stone; 68 were ceramic; 50 were glass. What significance can very simple artifacts like these have for the archaeologist?

Such a large and varied collection shows how many different varieties of marbles were made and used over the years. The time detectives know that certain types were made at different times, because of changes in the use of materials and

33

in methods of manufacture. They can use marbles to date other material found at the same site or in the same layer of soil. The earliest from Place Royale is a stone marble found in Champlain's Habitation, dating from about 1688.

Clues

How do archaeologists know how old something is? One way is to look closely at where it was found and what it was found with. When time detectives compare artifacts with other artifacts, or with features, whose ages are known, the technique is called relative dating.

Joseph Paradis in the eighteenth century should lie above them. Where would we find the plastic DC8? Since it is very recent it should be at the top.

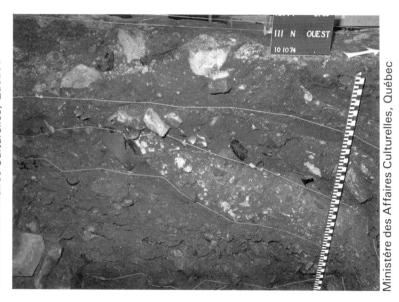

Ministère des Affaires Culturelles, Québec

Ministère des Affaires Culturelles, Québec

Stratigraphy describes layers of deposits or strata. It can help to date material. The site of the maison Paradis was first occupied by the Jesuit fathers in the seventeenth century. Therefore, the layer containing features and artifacts from this period should be at the bottom of the archaeologist's excavation. Remains from the time of

Seriation is a way of arranging a series of artifacts by changes in style or composition. At Place Royale marbles made of several materials were found. Stone marbles gave way to ceramic and these in turn were followed by glass. Archaeologists can arrange these finds to indicate which are older in comparison with the others.

Above, layers appear in excavation at the maison Paradis and are outlined for the photographic record.
At left, pieces of glass are used to date material from the same level since glass manufacture and the style of bottles has varied at different times.

34

Examples of each of the three types are counted. It is presumed that only a few of each type were made at first; the style grew in popularity and then faded as another took its place.

The graph could look something like this:

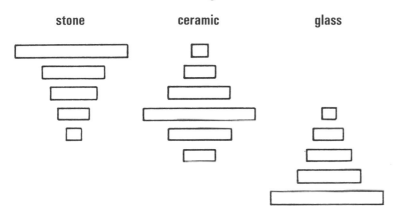

Since stone marbles are easiest to make, they were probably made earliest. Glass marbles require manufacturing skill and equipment and so were probably made the latest. As the popularity of glass marbles increased, the number of stone marbles grew less. You can see from the middle column that ceramic marbles overtook stone ones, then gradually gave way to glass.

Chemical seriation
Analyzing the chemical elements of an artifact may help the archaeologist to determine its age and also the source of the material from which it was made.

Pewter is a good example. It is made mostly of tin. The amount of lead in the mixture, or alloy, has varied at different times in the past. It was cheap to use but made the metal soft. Unfortunately, some manufacturers took advantage of this and made poor quality pewter. In more recent times, we have learned that the use of lead in food dishes causes health problems. As a result of both of these circumstances, regulations and laws were passed limiting its use. At the end of the nineteenth century in France and England the upper limit of lead in pewter was set at 10%. If chemical analysis of a food-related artifact (for instance, a plate or tankard) made in these two countries is found to contain more than that, it indicates an earlier date of manufacture. No lead is used now in pewter food ware.

Two laboratory methods which reveal chemical components are neutron activation analysis (NAA) and x-ray fluorescence analysis (XRF). Use of these methods is restricted because they are expensive and require specialists for their operation. They have been valuable in investigating metal artifacts whose composition has varied at different times and places of manufacture. NAA is especially useful where only a very small amount of a valuable artifact can be sacrificed for chemical analysis.

DOWN The Time Tunnel

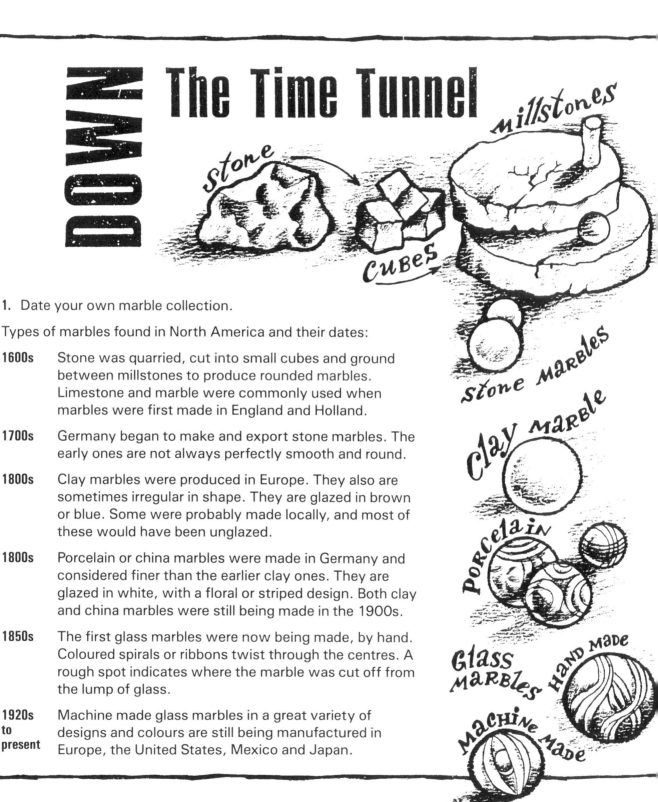

1. Date your own marble collection.

Types of marbles found in North America and their dates:

1600s Stone was quarried, cut into small cubes and ground between millstones to produce rounded marbles. Limestone and marble were commonly used when marbles were first made in England and Holland.

1700s Germany began to make and export stone marbles. The early ones are not always perfectly smooth and round.

1800s Clay marbles were produced in Europe. They also are sometimes irregular in shape. They are glazed in brown or blue. Some were probably made locally, and most of these would have been unglazed.

1800s Porcelain or china marbles were made in Germany and considered finer than the earlier clay ones. They are glazed in white, with a floral or striped design. Both clay and china marbles were still being made in the 1900s.

1850s The first glass marbles were now being made, by hand. Coloured spirals or ribbons twist through the centres. A rough spot indicates where the marble was cut off from the lump of glass.

1920s to present Machine made glass marbles in a great variety of designs and colours are still being manufactured in Europe, the United States, Mexico and Japan.

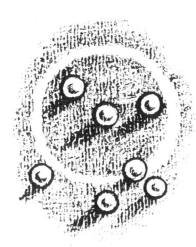

Ringer

hand's span

Bunny hole

2. The following marble games were played in Quebec. Similar ones are found all over the world.

Ringer
Draw a circle on the ground. Put a marble in the centre. Players take turns rolling their marbles along the ground trying to hit the target marble. First player to hit it three times collects all the missed marbles.

Bunny-hole
A more difficult variation of this game involves digging a small hole several feet away from a shooting line. Each player gets three tries to roll his marble into the hole. If the first player doesn't succeed, but the marble lands within a hand's span of the hole, the next successful player can claim it. If she or he does get the marble in the hole, the next player may knock it out and keep it. It takes skill and judgement to place your marble to the best advantage.

3. To find evidence of Champlain's Habitation in Place Royale archaeologists had to dig under the foundations of Notre-Dame-des-Victoires Church. Beneath the traces of the Habitation they found remains of an ancient First Nations burial.

The site could have looked like this.

The layers tell the story. Aboriginal people lived here first, followed by a European fortification. That was later demolished to make way for the church which we can still see today.

Tell the story of the site in this picture from the artifacts found in the different strata. Remember the bottom layer is the oldest. Who was living there first? What happened to them?

Crawford Lake

Ontario

Silent Waters straightened up. It was hard work chopping away at the thick log. His uncle, his teacher, had nearly hollowed out his end, his stone adze keeping a steady rhythm. They would fish together from this canoe. Silent Waters was nearly a man; he no longer helped his mother to grow corn and gather wild fruits.

From where he stood he could see her grinding kernels into flour outside the huge bark-covered longhouse. It was their home—at least, part of it was. They shared it with others of the Turtle Clan, his mother's family.

He smiled when his glance fell on his sister practising her pottery making. The bowls were small and uneven, and they didn't even have any decoration on them. Still, they were good for a girl as small as Clear Sky. Soon, he thought proudly, she would be making pots they could use.

"Look!" His uncle pointed.

Silent Waters turned toward the sparkling small lake. His father was coming out of the forest burdened with meat and a deerskin. Silent Waters ran to help him. There would be a feast tonight!

Something like this might have taken place 500 years ago on the shores of Crawford Lake in southern Ontario. The archaeologist-detectives uncovered the story because it is a very special body of water. Every year for thousands of years two types of sediments sift down through the water to settle on the lake bottom. In summer the layers are light-coloured from the chalk washed from the rock; in winter they are darker. A year's deposit of both colours is called a varve.

In most lakes sediments get mixed around when the water is disturbed by wind or changes in temperature. But Crawford Lake is small and very deep, and it is protected from winds by cliffs and trees. The top layer and the bottom layer of water do not mix. The bottom of the lake is stagnant, dark, cold and without oxygen. A lake like this is called meromictic.

There can be no life, not even bacteria, at the bottom of such a body of water. Since there is no decay, everything that falls is preserved—leaves, twigs, seeds, and even grains of pollen.

Archaeologists have many allies in the scientific world. In this case, Dr. Roger Byrne, now of the University of California, is a geographer and Dr. Jock McAndrews of the Royal Ontario Museum is a botanist, whose specialty is the historical and ancient green plant cover of southern Ontario. One of the ways they determine what that vegetation was in the past is by examining the sediments at the bottom of lakes to see what fossil plants they contain. An undisturbed meromictic lake is a rare and rich source of information.

At this site, Dr. McAndrews used the "frigid finger", an aluminum tube filled with dry ice (solid carbon dioxide) to penetrate the bottom layer. The mud around the tube froze solid and formed a crust. When it was removed, about 2000 years of sediments were revealed. The alternating dark and light layers of the annually deposited varves could be counted

Halton Region
Conservation Authority

Greg Stott

Opposite page above: Small, deep and secluded in its ring of trees, Crawford Lake conceals beneath its still waters secrets from centuries past.

Opposite page below: How many varves, layers of dark and light sediments, can you count on this sample from the bottom of the lake?

At right, Dr. Jock McAndrews of the Royal Ontario Museum, obtained samples of the sediments by lowering an aluminum tube filled with dry ice into the mud at the bottom of the lake. When the tube was pulled up a frozen crust showing the layers was carefully removed and stored in a freezer. The rubber glove attached to the top of the tube prevented water from entering but a small slit allowed gas to escape.

like the rings on a tree. What most intrigued the scientists was to find corn pollen in the mud dating between 1434 and 1459 AD. Somebody must have been growing a crop there very close to the lake. If this truly was the site of an aboriginal village, its age, during this twenty-five year period, is the oldest directly dated known in Canada.

The archaeologist-detectives were called in. Their mission was to find the site of the fields of corn. Dr. William Finlayson of The University of Western Ontario already knew that First Nations people had occupied the area because pottery and artifacts had been ploughed up. Now a farmer showed him a boulder, not far from the lake, that had never been moved. It was the stone used by the prehistoric village to grind—what else but corn!

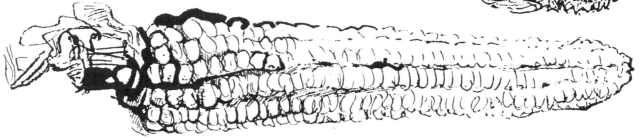

Halton Region Conservation Authority

Corn cobs, above, similar to those found at Crawford Lake. Note how much larger the modern one is.

The grinding stone at left, which gave a clue to the site, was used by First Nations women hundreds of years ago.

Opposite page: At left, marks in the soil—the remains of posts used in building—show the location of a longhouse when it was excavated. The reconstructed dwelling, shown at right, was erected on the original site. Drying racks for meat and fish stand in front.

Excavations by Dr. Finlayson's crews on the farm revealed the postmoulds of several longhouses which would have sheltered about 250 Iroquois-speaking people.

The features and artifacts recovered have formed the basis for a reconstruction of the village. Abandoned for 550 years, the village rose again on the exact location of its main structures. Two longhouses have been completely rebuilt and fitted out with reproductions of the original artifacts.

Halton Region Conservation Authority

Halton Region Conservation Authority

Clues

What is a natural clock?

The village site at Crawford Lake is very unusual, because the pollen core samples told very exactly the date when it was lived in, and when corn was growing in the fields close by. Like tree rings, the varves are natural clocks, a way archaeologists have of dating material.

Other Natural Clocks

Radiocarbon Dating

All living matter contains radioactive carbon-14 formed in the upper atmosphere. This carbon-14 is naturally converted into CO_2 gas, which is quickly incorporated into all living things. But, because carbon-14 is radioactive, it gradually decays once the living thing dies and can no longer get a new supply of carbon-14. By measuring the amount of carbon-14 left, the archaeologist can tell the time of death. It takes 5730 years for the amount of carbon-14 to drop to half its original level. So, if one quarter of the carbon-14 remained in an organic item, it would be 11 460 years old. This method can accurately date objects up to about 60 000 years old.

Potassium-Argon Dating

This method works in a manner similar to carbon-14

dating, but can only measure the age of rocks older than 250 000 years—useful for dating rocks with fossil remains.

The University of Toronto

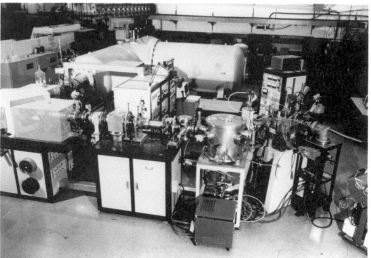

The University of Toronto

Thermoluminescence (TL)

This is a technique which measures the light released when a mineral crystal is heated. Crystals store energy they receive from background radiation at a constant rate. When a potter fires a clay object, the natural clock is reset: the energy stored throughout geological time is removed. The clock begins to tick again, storing energy that records the time when the pottery was made. When the archaeologist heats it again, perhaps thousands of years later, he or she can read this natural TL clock because the quartz crystals in the clay release some of their stored energy as measurable light. This thermoluminescent light can be measured by placing a photomultiplier over the heating sample. In principle, the archaeologist-analyst is completing an experiment begun hundreds of thousands of years ago by the potter. The more ancient the experiment, and the pottery, the brighter will be the TL light output.

Archaeomagnetic Dating

The direction and intensity of the earth's magnetic field has varied at different times. If a brick is heated and then cooled, the magnetic minerals within it will line up with the earth's magnetic field as it is at that time. Through the years that direction will remain the same, even though the magnetic field of the earth will have changed. The archaeologist can compare the direction and intensity of the artifact's magnetic field with those of the earth at different periods to find the time when it was made.

With delicate and complicated apparatus, scientists can read the age of ancient materials. At left is the University of Toronto's thermoluminescence laboratory, and above, the isotrace laboratory for radiocarbon dating.

DOWN

The Time Tunnel

sumac

purslane

1. Other seeds and pollen grains were found with the corn in the sediments at the bottom of Crawford Lake. These plants also were used for food by the village. Look in your backyard or a cultivated field for the wild vegetables Silent Waters and Clear Sky gathered for their mother.

Purslane and lamb's quarters grow as weeds from June to October. They are best in spring and early summer. Try purslane uncooked in a salad. Both lamb's quarters and purslane can be boiled with a little water and salt as green vegetables.

To make sumac "lemonade", gather the fuzzy red fruit clusters in the fall. Cover with water and bring to the boil. Boil for ten minutes. Strain off the reddish-brown liquid. Cool and add sugar to taste.

2. Many animal, bird and fish bones were also found on the site. White-tailed deer, gray squirrel and eastern chipmunk were the most common. Much bear meat was evidently also eaten. Sixty to seventy per cent of the bird bone appears to be from the now-extinct passenger pigeon.

Such remains, both animal and vegetable, are valuable clues for the archaeologist-detectives in reconstructing the way people lived on the site.

To find out what animals the bones come from, archaeologists compare them to skeletons in collections they can use as a reference.

You can form a reference collection. Gather bones from animals used as meat at home—chicken, pig, cow, fish. You may also be able to get parts of deer and other game skeletons.

Give each piece a number. Write it on the bone with India ink or a very fine tip drafting pen. Cover the number with colourless nail polish to keep it from rubbing off.

Enter the same number in a looseleaf notebook with a description of the animal and, if possible, note the part of the skeleton from which the bone came.

3. Corn and other crops, including squash and beans, are one of the important contributions First Nations people have made to our way of life today. The women were the farmers. After the men had cleared the land of trees, the women had control over seeding, caring for the plants and harvesting. Women were much respected in this society and had a strong voice on the village councils. Not only was corn a staple food, but the husks were used to make many articles, ranging from moccasins to masks. Clear Sky may have had a corn husk doll. They were popular in both First Nations and European cultures.

Save the husks and silk from cobs of corn.

Spread them to dry in an airy place for a few days before using. When you are ready to begin your doll, soak the husks in a basin of water for about half an hour. Keep them damp while you are working.

Besides the husks, you will need scissors, string and straight pins. If you use cornsilk or yarn for hair, you will need glue.

• Start your doll by picking out six large husks of good appearance. Tie them together tightly about 4 cm from the end. This knob forms the head. (Figure 1) Lift each husk in turn and pull it back carefully and firmly over the head. Smooth the surface and choose the best-looking side of this ball for the face. Now tie again under the head to make a neck.

• Take two long husks and roll them together, sideways, to form the arms. Separate the three back sections of the skirt from the three front pieces and insert the arms tightly up against the neck. (Figure 2) Tie around the waist to hold them in position.

• Fold two more husks, about 4 cm wide, to form shoulders. Cross these over the chest and back. Tie them in place with another string around the waist.

• To make an overskirt, pick out four or six good husks. (The number will depend on the size and quality of those in the underskirt). Arrange these around the waist of the doll and tie.

Cornhusk doll

Fig. 1

Fig. 2

Fig. 3

• Fold another husk about 3½ cm wide for a sash. Position this around the waist to cover the skirt seam and all strings. Tie the sash at the back and pin one end down over the other to keep it neat while drying. (Figure 3)

• The edges of the skirt should also be pinned together, one overlapping the next, so that they will dry in the correct position. You can stuff leftover husk up under the skirt to pad the hip section.

• Trim the skirt sections, if necessary, to a uniform length. Trim the arms also, if they are too long. Tie them at the wrist, about 1½ cm from the ends, to form hands.

To make a bonnet, cut a rectangle from a husk and shape it to the head. Fold and pin at the back.

• Cornsilk hair can be arranged and glued on when the doll has dried. Accessories, such as dried flowers or berries, can be glued on also.

• Carefully remove all pins when dry.

Tips:

If your husks are mottled, or if you would like your doll a uniform shade, they may be soaked in a mild borax solution for half an hour. Rinse them afterwards.

Tie string at all points as tightly as you can: the husks will shrink and loosen as they dry.

If any string shows, cover it with a strip of husk. Strips may be used instead of string, but are not as easy to work with.

Bend and pin or tie the arms in the position you want them as the doll dries.

A good idea is to rest your doll on an upended glass to dry. It may take a day or two to dry completely.

47

Lower Fort Garry

Manitoba

Frances Ross watched her brother, Donald, practising with his bow and arrows.

"Come away from the window, Fanny," said her mother. "Pick up your needle, now. We've got shirts to sew for Donnie and Roderick and dresses for you and Christy and Mary to take back to school. Look at Christy—she's got her skirt nearly finished."

Frances, or Fanny as the family called her, sighed, but picked up the shirt for 17-year-old Roderick. He was fussy these days. Not like Donnie, she thought. She sighed again at the thought of him out in the sunshine on the bank of the wide Red River.

Mrs. Ross sighed, too. "Finish that up and you can be away with Donnie this afternoon," she said.

A cough from the bedroom interrupted them.

"Go to your father, Christy, and see does he want a drink of water."

"I hope father gets well soon," said Fanny. "I like Norway House much better than here at Lower Fort Garry."

"Hush now. Don't disturb the poor man. He had a great deal of work and aggravation being Chief Factor of a busy Hudson's Bay Post. He's here to get some rest."

"Anyway," said Christy. "I like it at boarding school, Fanny, and so do Roderick and Mary. You should be thankful you can get an education."

Fanny made a face at Christy's back. She herself lived only for holiday times like now.

Life was so much easier at Norway House. She smiled, thinking of her Cree and Ojibway friends and the meals she had shared with them—delicacies like beaver tail and moose nose. Here, at Lower Fort Garry, they had to take tea with the Governor and his lady.

"The Big House is beautiful," she said, "but I wouldn't want to live there."

"You're not likely to, after dropping your cake on the carpet on Sunday," retorted Christy smartly.

"Fanny'd rather have pemmican and bannock with the trip men," piped up Mary.

"That's enough!" said Mrs. Ross. "Let me put that sleeve in again, properly, Fanny. You go and get two or three pails of water for dinner time."

Fanny fairly ran out the back door to the pump. The sun sparkled on the limestone walls of the fort and the red roofs of the buildings inside. Their own whitewashed cottage and the farmhouse and blacksmith's shone in the green spring field.

"Fanny!" called Donald. "Look. Boats coming in!"

She raced down to the water's edge. Loud laughter and shouting floated across the water—Cree, Ojibway, French, English, even Scots Gaelic, all jumbled together.

"Hello, Donnie! How is your father? Better, I hope, for he is good man."

"Aye, Donald Ross is the best Chief Factor of them all. Tell him we'll be up to see him before we leave for la Loche."

The oars were so long the men had to stand to push them forward, then sit to pull back. But they were so strong that the York boat, even fully loaded with furs, sped quickly to shore. Donnie grabbed the line and made it fast.

Louis Badone

The cottage where the Ross family lived, shown on this page, is small in comparison to the grand stone house (next page) built within the walls of the fort by Hudson's Bay Governor Simpson for his bride in 1830.

"Donald! Frances! Hurry up!" Donnie picked up his bow and arrows. Fanny retrieved the water pails.

"I'm going to be a trip man one day," said Donnie.

In 1850 when the Ross family lived at Lower Fort Garry, land at the junction of the Red and Assiniboine Rivers had already been used by fur traders for a hundred years. From here routes to the west and north led to regions which produced not only the best furs, but also abundant food in the form of buffalo meat. After years of fierce competition, the North West and Hudson's Bay Companies had combined and built a fort where the two rivers met. A flood had greatly damaged it in 1826. In 1830 the Governor of the huge area called Rupert's Land, which the Company controlled, decided to build a safer location twenty miles north, above the treacherous rapid.

Governor Simpson had a beautiful stone house built for his teen-aged bride, with all the luxuries that could be brought in to this wild country in the big York boats from York Factory on Hudson's Bay.

Louis Badone

York Factory was the place where the ships came in from England with supplies for the posts. And it was from there that the furs were shipped back across the ocean.

It has been said that Canada, the nation, was made by the beaver. Champlain built his fort in Quebec City to trade for furs. The maison Paradis was used by Pierre Allemand to store pelts in the 1680s. This trade was dependent on the great water routes to the interior.

The Nor'westers came in from Montreal by way of the St. Lawrence River to Lake Superior chain; the Hudson's Bay Company used the Hayes and Nelson Rivers.

From Lower Fort Garry brigades of boats set out each spring on the long, difficult journey to Lac-la-Loche to take food supplies and trade goods to the posts. They picked up the furs that each trader had collected from the aboriginal people and brought them out to the ships waiting at Hudson's Bay. Then they hurried to return to Lower Fort Garry with European goods before freeze-up.

Unfortunately for this lower fort, the site of the first Fort Garry right at the forks of the two rivers was a more convenient centre for traders. A new fort called Upper Fort Garry was built in 1836. The result—the birth of the city of Winnipeg. Although Lower Fort Garry was never as important, it did have a great role to play in providing food and other goods for the fur trade.

What did Frances and Donald do when they made their escape from chores on that spring afternoon nearly 150 years ago?

First they crossed the creek to visit the camp of their Cree and Ojibway friends. Many of the Hudson's Bay men had native wives. Mrs. Ross had come from Scotland as a child and although the Rosses did not have any native blood they knew their neighbours well and spoke both languages.

Donald and Frances stroked the stacked beaver pelts, the fox and other furs. Bags made of hide, full of pemmican, would soon be traded at the fort's saleshop. Pemmican was a very important food resource. Great herds of buffalo lived on the plains just to the west. There the Blackfoot nation had developed special skills of hunting them and drying the meat for pemmican which they supplied to the traders.

The screech of a saw and banging of hammers came from the other side of the creek where new York boats were being built for next year's brigade. Past there the children saw one of the oxen plodding to the blacksmiths for new shoes. He would need to be well shod to pull a Red River cart all the way to St. Paul, Minnesota.

Parks Canada

Beaver pelts, like this one stretched on a frame for drying, were prized in Europe because of the fashion for hats made from the soft inner hair. Trade for the beaver led to the opening of the continent to French and British settlement.

"Let's go to the bakehouse," said Donnie. He and Frances were always hungry. They ran along the river bank to the big front gates of the fort. Inside the walls stood the large and handsome Governor's house. Mrs. Colville and some ladies sat sewing in the flower garden.

In one corner of the inside wall was the building where the hardtack biscuits were baked. This type of bread kept well for months. The tripmen packed quantities of it, with pemmican, to feed them on their long journeys.

Fanny and Donald left a trail of crumbs on the way to the fur loft and sales shop where the boatmen would be. These were Donnie's heroes, the heroes of the fort, in fact of the whole Company. Strong and brave, tanned in the wind and sun, bold and free, they were the backbone of the fur trade.

Frances looked over at the summery flowered prints of the ladies' dresses. The men lounging on the steps of the stores were a hundred times more colourful. The Metis especially, in blue jackets with bright brass buttons, jaunty red caps, corduroy trousers, and of course moccasins. In winter they wore the trademark blanket coats and bright red sashes.

"So you want to come with us on the next trip, Donnie?" joked a bearded giant. "Better to stay at school. On just the Hayes river there are 34 portages! 34 times we have to pick up that boat, and all the goods, and carry them over the trail to the next bit of water."

"You heard about the bells for the Cathedral at St. Boniface, eh? 1600 pounds they weighed and we had to carry them over every one of those portages before we reached Lake Winnipeg. I think you wait a couple of years before you do that!"

But were not Greek, French, arithmetic, algebra and geography just as big a burden to 11-year-old Donald?

Visitors to Lower Fort Garry today can trace almost all of Fanny and Donald's tour on that spring holiday afternoon. Archaeology has helped to bring Lower Fort Garry to life again as it was in the 1850s.

The Hudson's Bay Company finally closed its store in 1911, and for the next 50 years the fort was used as a country club. In 1951, title to the property was given to the federal government, and restoration began in the 1960s to open it to the public. Between 1965 and 1967, 22 major excavations were made by the University of Manitoba. Archaeological work has continued under Parks Canada ever since.

When excavations began, the original walls of the fort, the bastions at the corners, and six other buildings were still standing, although they had been altered. Inside the walls, the ground had been disturbed by gardens, water and sewer pipes, electricity and telephone cables and roads. Outside the walls the land had been made into a golf course. Since it had

Five-foot squares were measured out for the excavation of the blacksmith's shop. A six inch baulk was left between squares to allow the diggers to move around.

On the plan below, drawn from the findings, can be seen remains of a stone forge built against the west wall.

To the right, based on the archaeology, is the present-day reconstruction of the blacksmith's shop.

Parks Canada

never been farmed there was no damage from ploughing, and it was much better preserved from change. Most of the structures in this area around the fort had fallen down or been moved away. Some foundations could still be seen.

Archaeological work was undertaken partly to aid in the restoration of the buildings within the fort. However, much work was also needed to provide information on what had stood on the grounds outside. The cottage the Rosses lived in was still standing, but changes had been made. Two seasons' digging revealed its original shape and construction.

Louis Badone

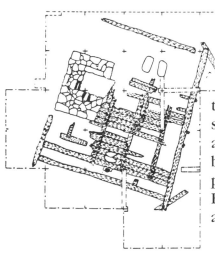

Only a small mound showed where the blacksmith's shop had stood. Excavation revealed an 18′ by 20′ log structure with a stone forge built against the west wall. Subsequent digs showed the location of the farm manager's house, the ox stable and other buildings. Archaeology played an important part in the restoration of the Big House, the blacksmith's cottage, and the Ross cottage.

Parks Canada

55

Clues

Before the archaeologist starts to dig, a map of the site is drawn up. A point (called the datum point) is chosen to act as a reference for all the measurements. On the site plan of Lower Fort Garry it is marked 0, near the north-east bastion of the fort, on the base line. The base line was established along the river side of the fort, oriented to the north and marked at 100′ intervals by steel pins.

With these in place, a grid system of squares could be laid out on the site—running at right angles and parallel to the base line. The squares are then given co-ordinate numbers. Often the datum point is se-lected as the start of the numbering system. A number-letter code is used, based on the compass points and the distance from the datum point. The first square south and west of the datum point would be S1 W1. Each square is exca-vated separately and material from it labelled with that num-ber.

By the use of grid plans and numbered squares, the archae-ologist keeps track of finds and can relate them to each other. Also, if it is necessary to go back to a certain area of the site for further work, it can be easily located within the grid through its letter-number iden-tification.

The archaeologist's plan of the site of Lower Fort Garry, showing the base line along the river, and the datum point marked "0".

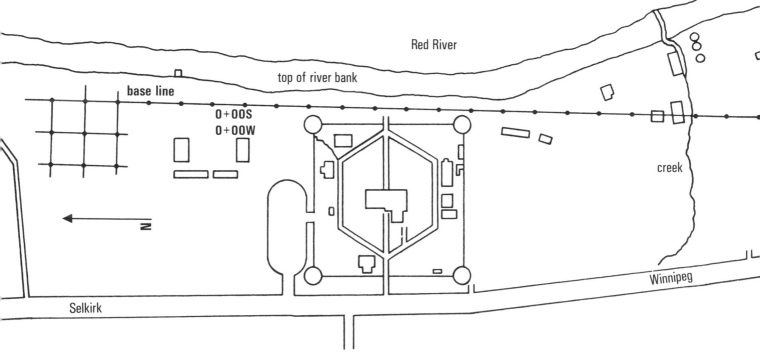

DOWN The Time Tunnel

1. At the age of 14, Donnie Ross went back to Norway House as an apprentice clerk for the Hudson's Bay Company. Fanny must have been pleased to visit him there. Find that post on the map. Why would it (and the other posts on the map) have been located where they are? Can you see where some of the portages would have to be made?

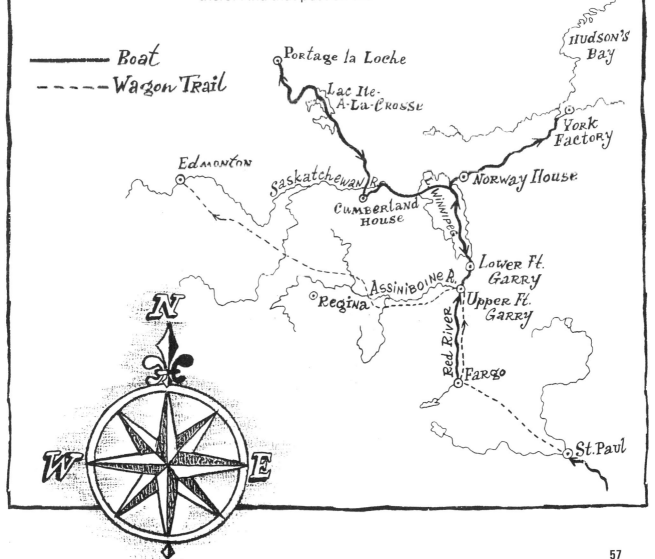

—————— Boat

- - - - - - Wagon Trail

Portage la Loche

Lac Ile-A-La-Crosse

HUDSON'S BAY

York Factory

Edmonton

Saskatchewan R.

Norway House

Cumberland House

Winnipeg

Lower Ft. Garry

Assiniboine R.

Regina

Upper Ft. Garry

Red River

Fargo

St. Paul

N

W

E

S

2. Weave a colourful headband or belt like the tripmen might have worn. You will need: three drinking straws, yarn, scissors, and a tape measure. Cut three 90, 120 or 150 cm lengths of yarn, depending upon how long you want your belt to be. Enough extra yarn for ties must be left at both ends.

• Thread a length of yarn through each straw.

• Tie a knot at the end of each piece of yarn so it will not slip through the straw. Cut a slit in the top of the straw and push the yarn down until the knot is caught and held.

• Hold the straws in your left hand with the knotted ends pointing up. This is your loom and these lengths of yarn are called the warp.

• Place a new piece of yarn from a ball of wool on top of the straws and hold it in position with your left thumb.

• Begin weaving this yarn, called the weft, with your right hand. Weave over and under, over and under the straws, going back and forth across the loom.

• Pull the yarn tight and push it down as you go.

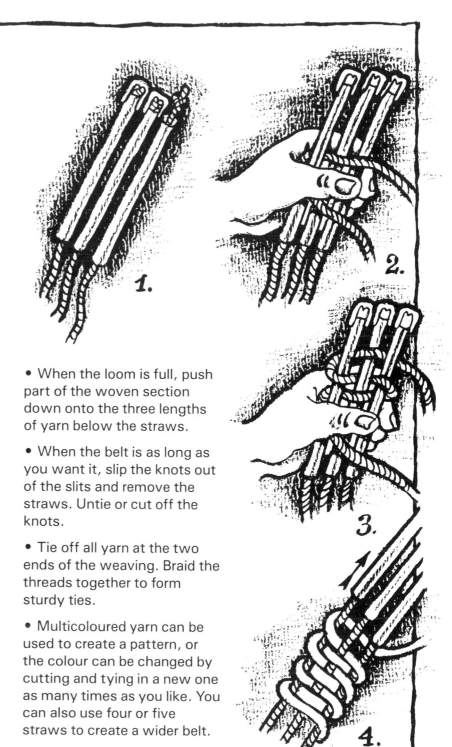

• When the loom is full, push part of the woven section down onto the three lengths of yarn below the straws.

• When the belt is as long as you want it, slip the knots out of the slits and remove the straws. Untie or cut off the knots.

• Tie off all yarn at the two ends of the weaving. Braid the threads together to form sturdy ties.

• Multicoloured yarn can be used to create a pattern, or the colour can be changed by cutting and tying in a new one as many times as you like. You can also use four or five straws to create a wider belt.

3. Canadian archaeologists use the Borden System to identify site locations in relation to the National Topographical Maps of the country. The Borden number for Lower Fort Garry is EaLf-29.

The topographical maps divide Canada into areas bounded by lines of latitude (the horizontal lines on a globe) and lines of longitude (the vertical lines on a globe).

The segments are identified by two capital letters. The first capital letter defines two degrees of latitude and runs from "A" to "U", starting at the southern boundaries of Canada. The second capital letter defines longitude from east to west.

Thus the "E" and "L" of the Lower Fort Garry Borden number tell us to look on the map EL of the National Topographic Series and this is bounded by latitude 50°N on the south and longitude 96° on the east.

The Borden System further divides the latitude and longitude letters in order to closely pinpoint sites. Lower case letters (the "a" and "f" of Lower Fort Garry's number) are used for these divisions within the large segment.

The last part of Lower Fort Garry's Borden number is "-29", and means that it is the twenty-ninth archaeological site to be found in that map reference area.

The Borden number of a site therefore tells us which map to look at, where to look on that map, and which site it is. The site reports will then locate each square in a dig to the base line and its datum point which ties back to Canada's mapping system. This means that future time detectives can go back to the exact spot even if it is now overgrown with trees or in a town.

What sites are represented by the following Borden numbers: Kk Do-3, Ai Gx-6, Ke Ve-2, Dk Pj-1?

What would be the Borden number where you live?

Borden System Site Identification Index Map

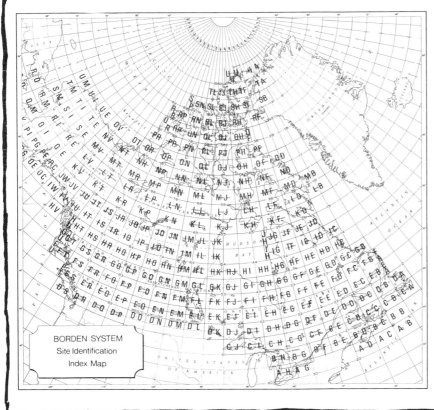

BORDEN SYSTEM
Site Identification
Index Map

Department of Mines, Energy and Resources

Head-Smashed-In Buffalo Jump

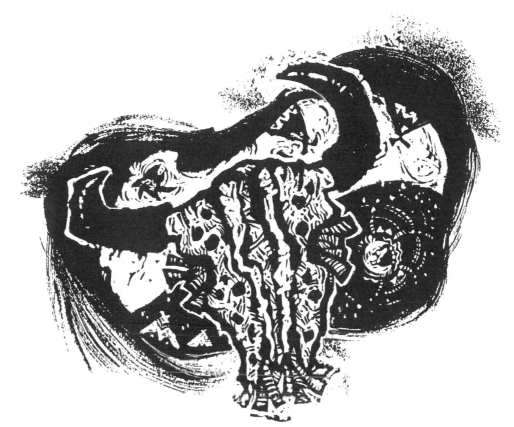

Alberta

Kit-Fox was crouched behind the "deadman". The cloud of dust rolling along the ground was getting closer. The buffalo were coming at last! She wondered where her brother was. Double Runner was one of the young men picked for strength and cunning who had found the buffalo and lured them here—to the edge of the cliff.

Beneath the soles of her moccasins Kit-Fox could feel the earth throb under the pounding of hundreds of hooves. The noise was all around her. Thudding, panting, grunting, screams and shouts of men and women. Suddenly, out of the confusion a buffalo raced toward her, away from the herd and its doomed path.

Kit-Fox stood, for an instant turned to stone like the deadman in front of her. Never had she seen anything so huge, with such a massive head and horns! Then she remembered what she was to do. Without the buffalo the Blackfoot could not survive. She forced herself to jump out from behind the pile of stones to try to divert the path of the charging beast.

61

"Go back!" she shouted. "Join your brothers!"

She waved her piece of hide almost in the animal's face. It stopped in its headlong dash, then swerved, foam whipping from its shaggy beard, hooves gouging the prairie sod.

Kit-Fox trembled like the earth, but she stood her ground waving and shouting to keep the mighty animals in a tight herd. It seemed like an eternity before an abrupt silence filled the drive lane at the top of the cliff.

She ran with the others to look over the edge. A mass of red animal flesh was piled up on the bloody rocks below. Hunters were spearing and shooting arrows into the buffalo that had survived the fall.

Down on the flats she saw the tipis of the camp. The butchering knives and cookers would be ready. There would be much work but much to celebrate, too, she thought. She felt a hand on her shoulder.

"You did well, Kit-Fox," said her mother. "The Medicine Lodge woman who named you after so powerful a helper will be proud of you."

Hundreds of years later, in 1987, their Royal Highnesses, the Duke and Duchess of York, officially opened the spectacular Head-Smashed-In Buffalo Jump Interpretive Centre. Built into the cliff face with descending levels resembling archaeological strata, it tells the story of this ancient site in southern Alberta. Why was it chosen, in 1981, for the select list of World Heritage Sites by UNESCO?

Archaeological excavations show that this place with its odd name was first used to kill buffalo about 5700 years ago. That makes it one of the oldest known jumps in North America. It also is one of the largest and the best preserved. But what is a buffalo jump and why is it called Head-Smashed-In? It should by rights be called a "bison" jump, since buffalo are only found in Africa and Asia. The first Europeans gave the animals of North America the same name because they reminded them of their own buffalo; the name has stuck. Whatever it is called, Kit-Fox and the people of the plains for thousands of years before her depended almost entirely on this animal for their

Built into the cliff face, Head-Smashed-In Buffalo Jump Interpretive Centre suggests the strata of an archaeological dig. This distinctive style is carried into the interior, where various levels tell the story of the site.

Alberta Department of Culture

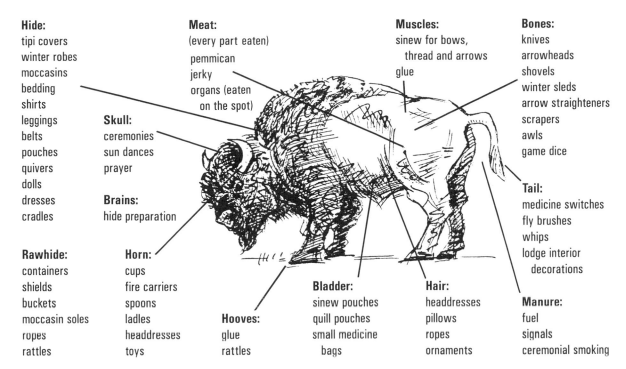

Hide:
tipi covers
winter robes
moccasins
bedding
shirts
leggings
belts
pouches
quivers
dolls
dresses
cradles

Skull:
ceremonies
sun dances
prayer

Brains:
hide preparation

Rawhide:
containers
shields
buckets
moccasin soles
ropes
rattles

Horn:
cups
fire carriers
spoons
ladles
headdresses
toys

Meat:
(every part eaten)
pemmican
jerky
organs (eaten
 on the spot)

Hooves:
glue
rattles

Bladder:
sinew pouches
quill pouches
small medicine
 bags

Muscles:
sinew for bows,
 thread and arrows
glue

Hair:
headdresses
pillows
ropes
ornaments

Bones:
knives
arrowheads
shovels
winter sleds
arrow straighteners
scrapers
awls
game dice

Tail:
medicine switches
fly brushes
whips
lodge interior
 decorations

Manure:
fuel
signals
ceremonial smoking

living. They ate its meat, used the hide for tipis and clothing, and the bones and horns for tools; even the tail became a switch used in the sweat lodge ceremony.

In ancient times, small numbers of bison were hunted with spears and darts. That way was dangerous and not always successful. However, if many could be killed at once, as happened at a buffalo jump, that would ensure that the whole tribe could live in comfort through another winter. Of course, the whole tribe had to work together—first to find the animals and then to drive them along the lanes marked out by stone cairns. When the herd was moving well, hunters would rush from behind to panic the animals into a headlong dash to the edge of the cliff—and over. Blindly, in a tight pack, they would hurtle together over the jump. Long ago, one curious young boy, who wanted to see the buffalo tumbling down the precipice, sheltered under the lip of the cliff to watch. The mass of animals soon overwhelmed him; when the others found him, his skull was crushed against the rock. Hence, legend tells us, the site was named Head-Smashed-In.

Three different areas make up the whole of the site. At the top of the cliff is a large grassy plain, ideal grazing land for the bison. The young hunters needed speed and endurance to urge the herd from this gathering basin into the drive lanes. At Head-Smashed-In these lanes extend about 15 km back from the cliff and follow the lie of the land between rises. They are marked by the deadmen, heaps of stones arranged in rows which funnelled the animals to the cliff edge. The second area is the kill site itself, at the bottom of the plunge. Here bones and stone tools have built up, layer upon layer, for thousands of years. The third region of interest is the camp site on the level plain beyond the kill.

Alberta Department of Culture

Alberta Department of Culture

Alberta Department of Culture

Archaeologists have examined all three in order to discover the size and age of the kill site, the methods of the hunters and the pattern of life in the camps.

Finding locations to dig was not a problem at Head-Smashed-In. The jump was a well-known local landmark. In fact, the first excavations were undertaken to preserve the kill site from the hordes of "pothunters" who scavenged for stone arrow points for souvenirs or to sell to collectors. More recently, attention has been focused on problems involving areas which could be in danger from the construction of the Interpretive Centre and its roads. Digs have also extended to the camp site to reveal information on how the bison were butchered. All the knowledge gained adds to the picture of the jump—who used it, and how it was used—that is presented in the Centre.

Much of the interpretation at Head-Smashed-In came from the work of historians and ethnologists, experts who study the way of life, or culture, of a group, in this case, the people of the Plains. Only in this part of North America were people so dependent on a single source for all their needs.

Kit-Fox was right in thinking that, without the bison, the Blackfoot would have difficulty in surviving on the great western grasslands. She knew that these animals were a gift from the creator, and that their trust and co-operation had to be won in special rites and ceremonies before they could be killed. The rituals before the present hunt must have been performed properly. If they had not, it would not have been such a success.

But they had been done properly and already the great slabs of meat were hanging on racks to dry. Soon she would be helping the women to pound it fine and mix it with fat and berries to make pemmican, the food which lasted for months and kept them through the lean winter.

Kit-Fox was glad that both she and Double Runner had done well in the hunt. She shuddered to think what punishment the members of the Warrior Society would have given them had they failed. Perhaps Double Runner would go on a Vision Quest now. Four days and nights without food or drink, alone on a high hill, only praying and singing songs, hoping to dream of a helper, perhaps an animal, to give him special power. Would he be able to endure? If he succeeded, he would be fortunate and perhaps become a member of the Warrior Society himself.

Kit-Fox had played a small but very necessary part in the great hunt. Everybody in the tribe had her or his special task, and sometimes two or three tribes worked together. It took a great deal of co-operation to organize everyone to obtain the meat and other essentials that would benefit them all. Perhaps one especially greedy hunter would kill a buffalo and butcher it for himself. This would threaten the success of the great co-operative hunt. Then the Warrior Society would have to act as policemen and punish his selfishness. In the same way they would have dealt with Kit-Fox or anyone else who did not do his or her duty to the tribe.

The most important religious event of the Blackfoot people, the ceremony of the Medicine Lodge, was held in the summer. This sacrifice to the great spirit, represented by the Sun, was offered only by women. A woman might make a vow to build a Medicine Lodge to ask for aid for a sick child or a son away at war. The rest of the people would move their tipis in a circle around the site selected for the Lodge. The woman herself had already collected at least a hundred buffalo tongues, considered the choicest part of the animal, and cut and dried them.

Prayers and songs asking the Sun for health, plenty of food, and success in war were offered. While these rites were being performed, the Medicine woman remained secluded and fasted for four days. Then the Medicine Lodge was erected and the woman entered.

At this time she cut up the sacred buffalo tongues and gave a small piece to every man, woman and child. They offered it first to the great spirit before eating it themselves. The Medicine woman who conducted these rituals was a greatly honoured and respected person.

Another part of the sun-dance was performed by some of the men to honour the great spirit. Sometimes vows had been made that if a relative survived an enemy attack or an illness, the men would hang at the Medicine Lodge. This meant that the skin of the chest was pierced with wooden skewers; then ropes were attached to the ends of the skewers. The ropes were tied to the top of a central post. The men sang and danced as they pulled away from the post until their flesh tore out. This was not a test of courage, but a thanks-offering or the honouring of a pledge.

The abundant supply of buffalo gave the people of the Plains the time and leisure to express their spiritual and artistic natures. The hunt brought them together and permitted the development of a unique culture.

How long did this type of society survive? The break-up began about 1750 with the arrival of horses from the Spanish colonies in the southwest. Individual hunters on horseback could pursue an animal much more easily now than those who still attacked on foot. The custom of banding together to hunt gradually disappeared. Less than a century later, Europeans had arrived with guns, and the slaughter began. Up to the 1860s, millions of buffalo in seemingly endless herds grazed the vast extent of the prairie grasslands. Today only a few small groups are left in parks set aside for the animals' preservation.

Clues

The crew uses everyday items to carefully uncover features and artifacts in their square.

Archaeological Resource Centre, Toronto Board of Education

After the archaeologist has measured the area into a grid system of units, as at Lower Fort Garry, digging begins. First, vegetation and debris from the surface are removed, often by shovelling. Each member of the digging crew has his or her own equipment. What kind of specialized tools do you think are used for excavating? The very ordinary, everyday items required include a trowel, a whisk broom, a dustpan or hand shovel, paint brushes, a two metre metal measuring tape and a pail. The blade of the trowel is scraped toward the digger, onto the dustpan or shovel. The earth is examined for artifacts; any found are recorded on maps and removed. Then the remaining dirt is put into the pail. If a larger artifact or feature is found in the ground, the whisk broom or paint brush may be used to clear the earth away from it.

At Head-Smashed-In some special problems were encountered. A great deal of the bison bone is badly preserved and fragile. Much would fall apart in the digger's hands unless very carefully excavated.

Each piece is mapped and drawn in its position before removal. It is also identified before it is moved—what bone it is, what part of the animal it came from. The archaeologists need a team of specialists—mapping experts, artists and bone experts—to help complete the picture.

Each square is dug to a depth of 10 cm at one time. All features and artifacts found to that level are recorded as a unit. The next unit will consist of the next 10 cm This will be repeated until no more material is uncovered or the archaeologist has found the answer to his or her question. If layers of natural soil or sediments are found, they are dug to the same 10 cm depth until the bottom of the layer is reached. Then the next soil level is kept separate and is excavated, like the upper layer, in 10 cm levels.

Most of the artifacts recovered at Head-Smashed-In are bones, stone tools and some pottery. Over 5000 stone points used to tip darts, spears and arrows have been recovered from the kill site.

Stone knives were used to cut up the meat. What the archaeologist finds today are the small flakes that came from the edge of the knife when it was sharpened. Most of the actual knives were taken away by the hunters to use again, although some, small and shapeless after much use, have been recovered here. Since the flakes were part of the original tool they can be a good clue to the way the meat was butchered. Analysis has been done on the blood residues found on these stone points. They have all proved to

be bison blood only, and some has dated back 5700 years.

Since these fragments of stone are very small, special care has to be taken in screening the earth from the excavation. When the pail of earth which has resulted from careful trowelling is full, it is carried to a screening device. All the earth is then sifted. At Head-Smashed-In, a very fine mesh is used to catch the stone flakes which are such tiny but important clues.

Archaeologists play an important part in telling the story of Head-Smashed-In Buffalo Jump to the world. Although they do not dig up ideas, they do uncover features and artifacts which confirm or add to the picture we get from legends and from historians and ethnologists. For example, at the top of a nearby hill, archaeologists have found the scooped-out areas where

Archaeological Resource Centre, Toronto Board of Education

Alberta Department of Culture

Above: Two crew members sift earth from their square through a screen to recover small pieces of artifacts.

Below: Excavated hearth with fire-cracked rocks and bison bones.

young men lay fasting on their Vision Quests. And from the bones retrieved at the base of the cliff, we know the age of the animal when it was killed. Calves are born in the spring and early summer. If young animals are involved we can judge what time of year the jump was used. Archaeologists also look at the teeth, and based on how worn they are, can tell the animal's age—just as a vet does with a horse.

At the campsite, numerous boiling pits were excavated. Bones were boiled by throwing red hot rocks into hide-lined pits filled with water. Marrow and fat extracted was mixed with the dried meat and berries to make pemmican.

All these archaeological findings tell us that Kit-Fox's life was rich materially and culturally. Perhaps she, in her turn, became an honoured and respected Medicine Woman.

DOWN The Time Tunnel

Buffalo Skull

1. Would ethnologists say that your society is organized like Kit-Fox's? Does everybody work together to obtain food and clothing, houses and utensils for all? How do you get your clothing? Where does your food come from? Can you obtain a house from the same place you get glue and knives? If your society is different, can you tell why?

Where does your food and clothing come from?

2. The buffalo skull was an important part of the Sun Dance ceremony. Sometimes it was elaborately painted. Do you know of any other symbols that distinguish a certain way of worshipping?

69

3. The tipi as a form of shelter shows an excellent use of the materials available to the Blackfoot people to fit the needs of their environment.

Women made the tipis and were the sole owners of them and all the family's household goods. Girls like Kit-Fox had play tipis and furnishings which they packed up, as their mothers did, and set up on a new site.

Originally, tipis were made of pieces of buffalo hide sewn together; later of strips of canvas. The cone shape deflected the worst effects of wind, rain and snow. Inside, they were roomy enough for comfort. The smoke hole allowed for good ventilation. The fact that they could be easily moved was a necessary feature for a hunting society which followed the buffalo herd.

Not all tipis were decorated. The design had to appear in a dream or vision. It might represent a historic event, or be a symbol of religious significance. These designs were believed to protect the family from illness or misfortune, and belonged only to that family. No one else would dare to copy or use them for fear of harm to themselves. The door of the tipi would always face east.

Often bands at the bottom and top of the tipi represented the earth and sky. Stars were shown by circles, and mountains by a row of points. Religious symbols from nature included rocks and thunder. Animals were often the sacred objects depicted, and of these, the buffalo was believed to be the most powerful helper.

A pattern for making your own tipi is shown. The shape has been compared to a cape with the smoke flaps forming a collar.

Material should be canvas or cotton duck, or any heavy, waterproof, synthetic fabric. Smaller models could be made of fabric or heavy paper. You will also need poles, and rope for tying them together.

Lacing pins to close the front edges can be made of pointed sticks or dowel. Wooden pegs can be used to anchor the tipi at the bottom.

Since the dimensions are in metres, you can make larger or smaller tipis by multiplying or dividing the figures on the pattern as follows:

- Full size
  Blackfoot tipi   Multiply by 2
- Floor size
  toy tipi   Divide by 10
- Table top
  model   Divide by 20

Poles required:

	Number	Length
• Play tipi	11	3.5 m
• Full size	22	7 m
• Floor size	11	0.35 m
• Table top	11	0.18 m

For a full size tipi, wooden poles should be 80 mm in diameter at the butt end, 40 mm at the tie point.

Bamboo garden pole or wooden dowel (40 mm in diameter) could substitute in the play and floor sizes. Branches or even wire could be used in the table top model.

For a play tipi you will need about 30 metres of material one metre wide. A full size tipi will take about double that.

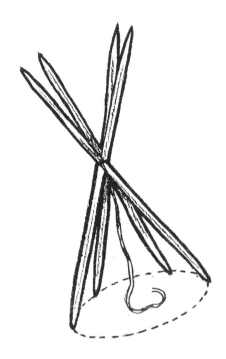

Method:

• Lay the pattern on fabric. Depending on the width of your material, you will need two or three strips of differing length. Cut and sew these together, removing excess fabric.

• Sew a 0.18 m wide hem down both front edges. Make holes for lacing pins through the hems.

• To erect the tipi, lay four poles on the cover, two crossing over two, and tie them where they will meet at the top of the tipi.

• Stand them up at equal distances apart. Lay in the other poles at the crotch. (See diagram.) Let the end of the rope hang near the centre of the floor and anchor it there with a peg.

• Now lay the lifting pole on the reinforced area of the cover and tie the tapes of the tie flaps securely to the pole. Fold the cover into a bundle and hoist the lifting pole to its place at the back of the tipi. Bring the two edges of the cover around to meet at the door. Spread poles out at the base so that cover fits snugly. Insert lacing pins.

If you are going to decorate your tipi, what symbols from your culture could you use to help and protect you?

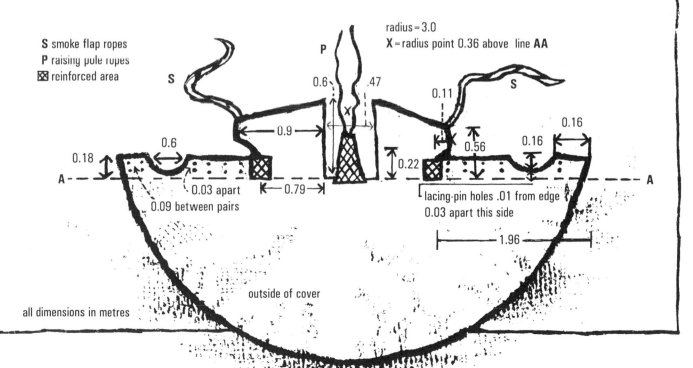

S smoke flap ropes
P raising pole ropes
⊠ reinforced area

radius = 3.0
X = radius point 0.36 above line **AA**

outside of cover

all dimensions in metres

British Columbia

Nekt, the fierce Gitksan warrior lord, pulled on his heavy armour of grizzly bear skin lined with pieces of slate. This time it was the Haida from the Pacific coast who were trying to dislodge him and his band from his fortress atop the hill at Kitwanga. They thought they could take control of the trade up and down the Skeena River from him, Nekt, the most powerful chief in the region! He looked down contemptuously at the warriors gathering below to attack. His men were ready with bows and arrows; he had his magic club, called Strike-only-once, for it found its mark every time.

The women and children were crowding into the secret hiding place under the floorboards at the back of the houses. They would lie motionless there listening to the uproar of the battle above, ready to bolt down the escape tunnel if the Haida broke into the fort. No time now for more preparation. The Haida were advancing to the slope.

"To the walls!" shouted Nekt.

Each Gitksan warrior ran to stand by his particular length of cedar root rope which held heavy spiked logs in position. The Haida were charging forward up the hill.

Nekt blew the signal on his war horn.

The ropes were slashed through in an instant. The logs rolled down slanted poles, crushing and maiming the first line of Haida, throwing the men on the others behind.

With a wild rush Nekt and his Gitksan warriors leaped down the hill, clubbing some of the enemy and shooting arrows at those trying to flee.

It was a triumphant feast Nekt and his followers held that night in the Ta-awdzep (fortress) at Kitwanga.

Opposite page: This totem pole depicts the story of Nekt. Carved in the canoe are Nekt's mother, Lutraisuh, and Nekt himself, as a baby, facing the head of his father.

At far right: A replica of a copper ceremonial shield marks the site of the Battle Hill.

This fort was only one of many that controlled trade up and down the rivers that flowed from the interior of northern British Columbia to the Pacific Ocean. Each had its chief and warriors who were prepared to do battle for power and prestige.

But only at Kitwanga and its neighbouring fort at Kitselas on the Skeena River were the stories of the ancient wars and battles recorded. The life of Nekt was the stuff of legend. His mother, Lutraisuh, was carried off by a Haida chief in a raid which had resulted in many deaths. Her new husband killed

Louis Badone

their first two sons, fearing that they would some day avenge their uncles, her murdered brothers. When Nekt was born, his mother tricked her husband into believing the baby was a girl, and it was allowed to live. But Lutraisuh, with the help of the Haida women who were sympathetic to her, resolved to take the baby back to her people. She slew her husband while he slept and cut off his head, which she took with her in the canoe the women had supplied. On the long, hard journey to the mainland, her son is said to have suckled the protruding tongue of his father's head, and so he got his name, Nekt, or Tongue-licked. They reached safety and were taken in by relatives.

But Nekt was always wild and reckless, even killing other youths. Eventually, he and his mother were shunned and forced to take to the woods. Nekt banded together with other outlaws to raid nearby settlements, and established their head-quarters at the Fortress. With his grizzly bear armour and magical club, Nekt attained mythical stature. But eventually it was realized that he was only human and his enemies finally found a way to overcome him. Nekt was shot, some say, by the first gun ever seen in that country.

Stories abut Nekt were first collected from the Tsimshian people and written down over 50 years ago by the Canadian ethnologist, Marius Barbeau, aided greatly by William Beynon, one of whose parents was Nishga, neighbours of the Gitksan. Many years later Marius Barbeau told the tales to Dr. George MacDonald, now the Director of the Canadian Museum of Civilization in Ottawa. Dr. MacDonald heard about Kitwanga again from Mrs. Polly Sargeant of Hazelton: her Skeena River Totem Pole Restoration Society had decided to erect a historical marker at the Fort. In 1975, the Battle Hill was made a National Historic Site, one of the first to commemorate native culture.

Louis Badone

Only rarely is it possible to examine a site with so many years of native history behind it. Dr. MacDonald undertook a dig in 1979. Once again the hundreds of manuscripts of Marius Barbeau were consulted at The Canadian Centre for Folk Culture Studies, and First Nation research assistants were hired to advise on planning the excavation and to help explain obscure features or artifacts.

Would the archaeologist's findings bear out the story of Nekt and his fortress on the hill?

Dr. MacDonald saw ridges of earth which clearly outlined the walls of a house. His first test dig was in one of the side walls, the second in what was thought to be the hearth area. Eventually house support posts and food storage pits were uncovered. At the back of the house was a large pit which later was found to lead under the back wall and the palisade— probably the hiding place and escape route for women and children. In all, five plank houses were excavated. The first one appeared to belong to a chief, since it had a sunken area surrounded by benches and a wide platform at the rear which could be partitioned off—features known to belong only to persons of importance. Likely this was Nekt's house.

Some of the food storage pits uncovered were used in the preservation of fish and related to the trade in food which the forts commanded. The oil from the eulachon, a small fish from the Nass River area, was an important part of the diet of the people.

New trade goods, including prized iron and copper, appeared about 1700, when English and Spanish ships came from the south and the Russians established posts in Alaska to trade for furs from the interior. Forts such as Kitwanga brought great wealth and power to the chiefs who claimed ownership of trails and bridges in their territories and demanded fees for their use. Nekt was not the only warrior lord to raid other villages for slaves and property.

In confirmation of the Gitksan stories, Dr. MacDonald found large pieces of charcoal, evidence of the burning of the fort. Tree rings from the charcoal compared with living trees at the site show that it was destroyed in the 1830s, at about the time the Hudson's Bay Company established trading posts in the area. Guns then made their first appearance. Very likely they were connected with the end of the fortress and the end

Opposite page: Stone war club used in battle.

of Nekt himself. His enemies now were able to shoot into the fort from nearby hilltops; they no longer had to try to scale the slopes in the face of the log defences.

Although Nekt and his fort were gone, some of his followers survived and moved to the present village of Kitwanga. The name of Nekt still exists in the area today.

Artifacts found at the site included a cache of arrows and spears. In another closely related site, slate dagger blades, and massive stone clubs shaped in a wide range of animal figures, were discovered. Stories tell of 18-foot long poles with knives or spear points lashed to the ends. "War picks" consisted of a stone blade fastened to a wooden or bone handle. Dr. MacDonald notes that skulls found in an adjacent area (Prince Rupert) have holes from just such a weapon. Nekt's Strike-only-once club was probably one of these.

Sometimes champions would be picked to fight in single combat. As in medieval Europe, the outcome of the duel determined the success or failure of the whole band. Likewise, combatants wore armour. Like Nekt's grizzly bear hide with pieces of slate glued into position, many were made of leather. Some were made of wooden slats. Wooden helmets carved with fierce human or animal faces protected the warriors' heads.

Clues

What does the archaeologist do with artifacts such as these to preserve them and make them available for future use? First, they require great care in excavation. When an object first appears the archaeologist must check to see if it can be safely removed. A fragile article may need a resin or wax spray to hold it together. Before it is removed, it is often drawn or photographed. After carefully noting its position, the excavator will brush or wash the piece and place it in an appropriate container. If it is small, like a pottery sherd or a bead, it is put into a paper bag. Clear plastic boxes and corrugated cartons are used for larger objects. Delicate items may be packed in cotton wool, tissue or styrofoam. Each container will be labelled with necessary information. The contents are described, and, along with their location on the site and within their square, the name of the digger and the date are noted.

Often a small laboratory is set up on the site. When the artifact arrives its tag is checked and it is cleaned and given a number. An artifact card with detailed information, a photograph and notes of any necessary treatment is then made out. Later, broken objects may be reconstructed.

Wooden objects must be kept wet or they will split and warp. Dr. MacDonald dug a site at Prince Rupert Harbour where over 400 artifacts were preserved underwater. After careful cleaning in the field each piece was sealed, in water, in plastic tubing and shipped to the laboratory in Ottawa. There it was rinsed and placed in a solution which cleaned it and slowly impregnated it with wax. It might take a year before the wax is absorbed and the wood consolidated.

Artifacts of other materials need different care. Metals should be kept dry; bone can be washed, but ivory can be dry-cleaned only.

Finally, the artifacts, carefully catalogued and conserved, can be organized according to what they were used for, how they were made, and in what style. Then the archaeologist can read the story of the way of life of their owners.

Archaeological Resource Centre, Toronto Board of Education

Archaeological Resource Centre, Toronto Board of Education

Kitwanga

This double mask, called Broken by the Sun, at right, was carved in 1908. The outer being is blind. The performer would open and close the mask during ceremonies while a singer chanted the words "the sun will shine on me and break through."

A wolf headdress, below, has abalone-shell inlay. The wolf house also lived in the fortress on the Battle Hill and later moved to Kitwanga village.

Canadian Museum of Civilization

Canadian Museum of Civilization

From Kitwanga, a marvellous collection of objects of great beauty has been preserved to help tell the story of how the Gitksan people lived, a century and more ago.

Joanne MacDonald, formerly of the Ethnology Division of the National Museum of Man, examined museum collections of objects connected with the people of Kitwanga. Her work has been published by Parks Canada in *Gitwangak Village Life: a Museum Collection*. Many of these artifacts are intricately carved and painted masks. Some represent the animal crest of a house, or clan. Nekt's were the frog and raven, but he had also won the eagle from another clan.

Other masks showed the connection between either a shaman or a chief and the spirit world. In the Gitksan view, humans share the universe with other beings. The non-humans are superior in ability and knowledge and so are more powerful. However, when Raven released the sun into the sky the other world was at a disadvantage, endangered by daylight. Eventually some humans were allowed to acquire some supernatural abilities and knowledge. This made them powerful but was in turn dangerous to them. Contact with non-humans could lead to a complete loss of humanness, the equivalent of death. Both men and women could be shamans. Their powers were individually acquired, while a chief's powers stayed with his house and could be inherited. Names, songs and theatrical presentations went with the masks. Since their power was so great they were only revealed to all the people at ceremonies, usually held in the fall and winter, sometimes to initiate people into secret societies. By acting out their legends and beliefs the people kept them alive for the next generation.

79

DOWN The Time Tunnel

Make your own mask and try to show what special power you would seek from the spirit world.

You will need:

• a paper bag or cardboard (corrugated cardboard from cartons is sturdy and flexible)
• scissors
• paints, foil, coloured paper, and yarn for decoration
• glue
• string

Paper Bag Mask

Pull the bag over your head and cut it so that it fits comfortably on your shoulders. Have someone carefully mark where you will want holes for eyes and cut the holes out. Draw your design on the bag. Paint. You can also glue on coloured papers, strips for whiskers, foil and feathers, yarn for hair or anything else you think is interesting.

Cardboard Mask

Cut a piece of cardboard big enough to wrap around your face. Make it any shape you want—square, oval, round, with animal ears or perhaps a pointed beard.

Position it on your face and have someone mark where the holes for eyes and mouth, and a flap for your nose, should go.

Cut out holes and flap.

Paint and decorate as for the paper bag mask. Make holes at sides above your ears for string ties. Knot string after pulling ties through holes.

Paper Bag Mask

Cardboard Mask

Cardboard Mask

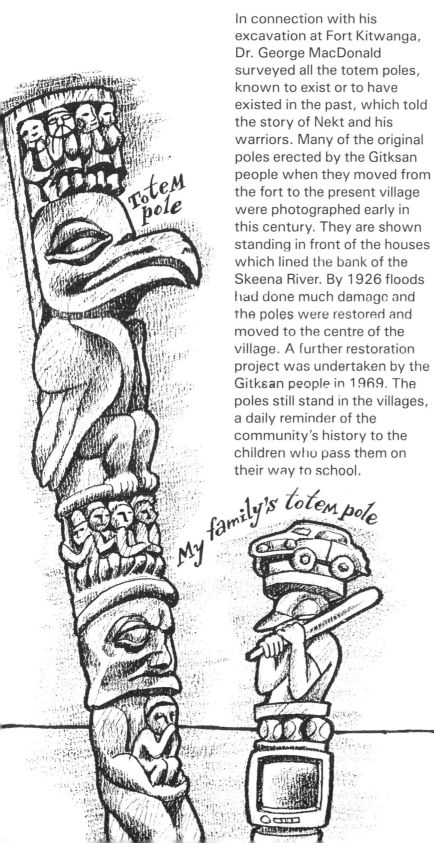

totem pole

My family's totem pole

In connection with his excavation at Fort Kitwanga, Dr. George MacDonald surveyed all the totem poles, known to exist or to have existed in the past, which told the story of Nekt and his warriors. Many of the original poles erected by the Gitksan people when they moved from the fort to the present village were photographed early in this century. They are shown standing in front of the houses which lined the bank of the Skeena River. By 1926 floods had done much damage and the poles were restored and moved to the centre of the village. A further restoration project was undertaken by the Gitksan people in 1969. The poles still stand in the villages, a daily reminder of the community's history to the children who pass them on their way to school.

Louis Badone

Each figure on the pole represents a part of that story. The Gitksan people traced their descent through their mothers. Women and men had equal powers as shamans and sub-chiefs. The totem poles tell the story of the possessions and events in the life of a family. What would you want carved on your family's pole? Ask your parents and grandparents what they would consider important.

Draw and paint your own totem pole.

Ruth Gotthardt

Bluefish Caves

Yukon

A small dark figure dressed in skins, carrying a stone-tipped spear, crept cautiously to the rim of the ridge and looked over. Quickly he beckoned to his companions. Here was their prey—a huge brown mound of fur with two giant tusks—what we now know as a woolly mammoth. It bellowed. Perhaps it had fallen and was in pain, thought the hunter. It made little difference, the animal would probably not be dangerous. They had ventured so far following the animals that here, in this strange land, the beasts did not yet know that human beings were hunters. The little band moved in for the kill, their few hundred pounds pitted against the mammoth's massive bulk.

In the Bluefish Caves of northern Yukon, near the village of Old Crow, archaeologists have found over 10 000 animal bones, probably left by human predators. Among the mammoth bones is one broken by a heavy blow, likely from a rock. The bone radio-carbon dates to 15 000 BP (before present). Was it a human hand that smashed that bone and sucked the marrow out?

There may be evidence here of the first appearance of human beings in the Americas.

Where did this hunting group come from?

During the last ice age, between 25 000 and 12 000 years ago, ice sheets covered most of Canada. But Alaska, Yukon and parts of nearby Siberia were too dry to form accumulations of snow. Separated now by the Bering Strait, the area then was one vast tundra plain with vegetation to attract grazing animals. Scientists believe that human beings, thousands of years ago, followed the herds in their quest for food, from Asia across the Bering Land Bridge and so into the New World.

What did the archaeologists find at the Bluefish Caves to help support this theory?

Test excavations in the late 1970s yielded large quantities of well-preserved remains.

Dr. Jacques Cinq-Mars of the Canadian Museum of Civilization has been digging in the area for several years. He and his colleagues first realized the importance of their finds in the caves when some of the bone uncovered proved to be from horses. Horses, and some other mammals (among them mammoths, mastodons and camels), became extinct in the Americas at the end of the last ice age, 10 000 years ago. Archaeological material dating back to this period would be the oldest yet found in Canada.

Were there also indications that humans were connected with this hoard of fossilized animal bones? It seems improbable that any other predator could be responsible for such a large accumulation.

In addition, in the upper stratum of the deposits, dating from 10 000 to 13 000 years ago, some artifacts chipped from flint were found. These stone tools are similar to those found of that date in Siberia. Bones recovered from this level show marks of tool use in butchering.

Evidence in lower, older levels (dating from between 15 000 and 20 000 BP) is slighter. Tiny flakes of flint, which could have been struck off in the manufacture of tools, and some nicks on bones, are suggestive of human activity. A cobble hammerstone was also found on the bedrock at the base of the excavation.

Ruth Gotthardt

Ruth Gotthardt

Bones of horses, bison, camels, mammoths and mastodons (at right) were found in the caves.

Stone tools and flakes of flint, below, indicated the presence of human beings.

These dates would indicate that, thousands of years before the pyramids of Egypt were built, Stone Age hunting groups from Siberia began to fill the immeasurable emptiness of the American continents.

If you tried to make the tipi described in the last chapter you followed a process known to archaeologists as replication. That is, trying to reproduce an artifact in the way that it was originally made by the people whose way of life is being studied.

What value could copying an object have for archaeologists? Firstly, it shows how much skill and knowledge the maker must have possessed. Secondly, the reproduction can be put to use. The original must be saved, but the copy can be experimented with. The most common form of replication is flint-knapping, or the making of stone tools.

Two methods were commonly employed to produce a projectile point. First, percussion was used. A hammerstone was struck against another piece of rock to flake off a piece of a suitable size and shape.

To thin and shape the point further, pressure was then used. A piece of antler or fire-hardened wood was pressed hard around the edges of the stone tool. Further refinement produced a finished fluted point.

The archaeologist can test the copy in the ways the original might have been used. Is it sharp enough to cut? How deeply does it cut an object? What causes it to break? Where does it wear down? Examination of the wear marks on the edges can tell archaeologists what material a tool could cut, for example, meat or hides. It can demonstrate how the original owner used a tool and what he or she could do with it.

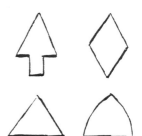

Clues

basic shapes

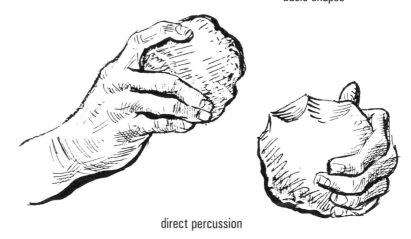

direct percussion

pressure flaking

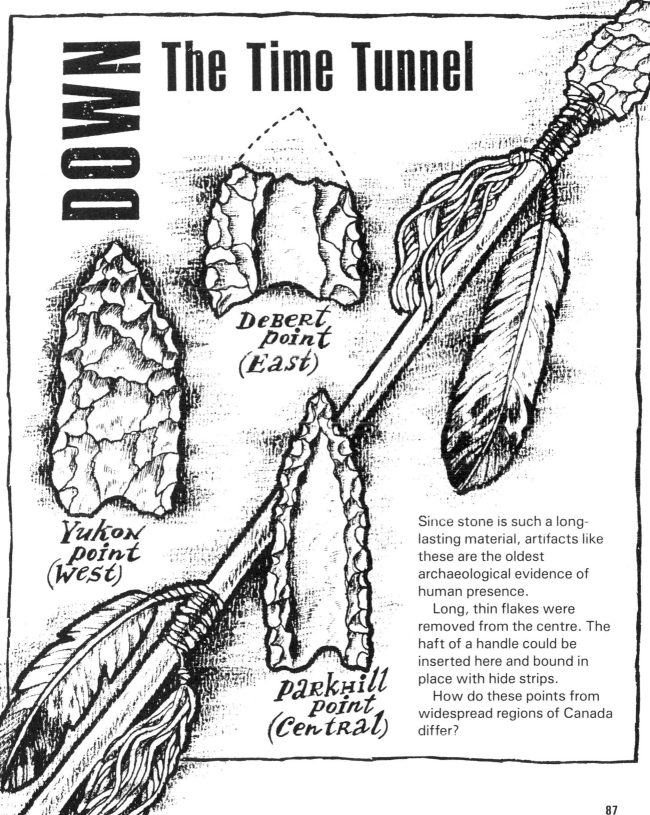

DOWN The Time Tunnel

Debert point (East)

Yukon point (West)

parkhill point (Central)

Since stone is such a long-lasting material, artifacts like these are the oldest archaeological evidence of human presence.

Long, thin flakes were removed from the centre. The haft of a handle could be inserted here and bound in place with hide strips.

How do these points from widespread regions of Canada differ?

87

Ruth Gotthardt

Fort Selkirk

Yukon

Much further south in Yukon, at Fort Selkirk, another archaeological project was undertaken.

The Selkirk First Nation felt a need, a few years ago, to find out more about their history and traditional culture and to record these things—especially for their young people. Since there were few written accounts, information had to be obtained from oral histories and from the clues that archaeologists could uncover.

Members of the group, with the help of the Yukon Heritage Branch, contracted with two archaeologists to set up and supervise the dig. Many elders, both women and men, were involved in contributing their knowledge of the past. Pelly Crossing high school students formed the field crew. A course was designed to give the students instruction in Yukon prehistory and the basic principles and techniques of archaeological excavation. The high school has developed some of this material with a view to using it for a credit course.

The students worked on the excavations in the morning. In the afternoon they listened to the elders talk about people who had lived at Fort Selkirk and how they had made their living. They knew the location of former hunting and fishing camps.

Ruth Gotthardt

The elders also contributed their knowledge of the old ways of making bows and arrows, snares for small animals, and bone tools for scraping skins. Replicas of these and other articles, including a fish spear, fish traps, a birch basket and a bark baby carrier, were made to demonstrate, and perhaps preserve, some of the traditional techniques.

Ruth Gotthardt

In most other archaeological excavations, the field crew is digging up the material remains of a culture which is not its own. At Fort Selkirk it was the people who now live in the area who were investigating their own past. They wanted to know what had occurred on their land, and how their ancestors had lived.

Opposite page above: elder Mrs. Kitty Jonathan shows Eugene Alfred how to make sinew, while Bernice Johnny works on a birch bark baby carrier.

Opposite page below: A crew reconstructs a fish trap, helped by elder Stanley Jonathan.

Below: Lynda Joe and Bernice Johnny excavate a 3000-year-old site near Fort Selkirk.

Ruth Gotthardt

What did the student field crew discover? The type of stone tools found at one end of the town site indicate that here was a traditional campsite that had been used, off and on, for 5000 years. How many people can say that they know exactly where their ancestors lived 5000 years ago? Can you?

Charcoal from another area dates from between 350 and 100 years ago. Remains from many occupation levels here agree with oral accounts that it was used as a salmon fishing camp.

Fort Selkirk also appears to have been an important prehistoric trading site. Twenty-eight different types of stone, as well as native copper, were recovered here. Many of these, since they are not found locally, would have been obtained in trade from neighbouring groups.

Evidence of fishing and hunting activities was found at a number of sites. At Three Way Channel, remains of fish baskets and a weir were recovered. Stone chips and flakes were found on a rock outcrop known to the elders as a lookout for game. No doubt hunters in the past sharpened their tools as they waited and watched.

Historic non-native sites included mine workings and the remains of the first Hudson's Bay post on an island at the mouth of the Pelly River.

A much more complete picture of the history of the Selkirk people and of the area has begun to emerge. It is one which the young people have discovered themselves and which gives them a strong sense of their place in the continuity of their culture.

The partnership of the archaeologists and the Selkirk First Nation storytellers has proved its value. Much information has been obtained and preserved. The curiosity, traditions and oral history of the native people joined with the techniques and experience of the scientists has revealed a more complete picture for future generations.

Clues

One of the requirements of the student field crew members was to make a record of all the artifacts and features uncovered as they excavated their squares. Even very small pieces of objects must be noted. They may be connected with a find in another square and prove to be just the bit which holds the key to a mystery.

Keeping an accurate record of each day's findings is vital. Without the record the dig is just a hole in the ground. The completed record forms contain the basic information the archaeologist needs to make sense of his or her findings, to form a view of events and activities—in other words, to interpret the site.

The forms are filled out at the end of each day's work when all the details are still fresh in the crew members' minds. A day or so later it's much harder to remember the exact position of an artifact in the square, or just how deep it lay.

Graph, lined and blank paper are necessary to make a complete record of an excavation.

Stratification is plotted on graph paper. Here the layers in the profile of a wall are shown.

Graph paper is also used to indicate the location of artifacts and features in a square.

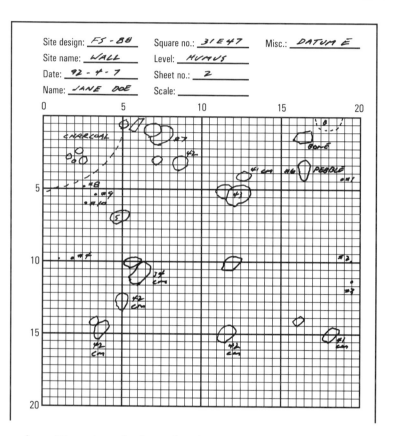

A written description of artifacts and features is put on lined paper or on a printed form.

In addition, drawings are made of features, artifacts in position, and of the different strata uncovered.

Photographs are taken of important objects before they are removed, and of any feature of special interest.

Artifacts found in each level are listed in numerical order, usually on a special form. They are described briefly, and their position and depth in the square noted.

Each layer or feature in a square has a separate record. All the forms will have the site number and name and the date and excavator's name, as well as the unit number and the layer or feature designation. At the end of the day the site supervisor collects all the records. Later on, when they are examined by the archaeologists, and records of adjacent squares put together, the whole picture of the site emerges.

When several squares are uncovered we can see that a brick wall carries on in its neighbour to the east, but not to the west.

When the diagrams are put together, perhaps the paving stones that look like a doorsill will prove to be a longer walkway.

Louis Badone

Without accurate records, the story may never be complete.

EXCAVATION RECORD

Site _KkDo-3_ Feature # _40_ Grid Unit _So Wo_ Date _92-7-23_
Excavator _JOHN DOE_ Feature _HOUSE_ Level _3_
Grid Unit Elevations: SWC_____ High Point_____
Level Depths:_____ to_____

	Field #	Coordinates	Depth	Description
A	15	S1.65 W1.39	-.96	CHERT FRAG
R	16	S1.64 W1.34	-.95	" "
T	17	S1.00 W1.06	-.96	" "
I	18	S1.13 W1.05	-1.02	SLATE
F	19	S1.16 W1.15	-1.01	"
A	20	S1.02 W1.21	-1.02	CHERT
C	21	S1.40 W1.00	-.99	CHARRED WOOD
T S	22	S1.36 W1.02	-1.00	GROUND SLATE

DOWN The Time Tunnel

1. Often what an archaeologist uncovers is not a complete artifact or feature but only an indication that something had existed in that place at some time in the past. Wood, for instance, once rotted, leaves a characteristic dark stain in the earth. This experiment will show you how the traces of a material will appear in an excavation.

You will need:

• two empty one-litre milk cartons
• sand to fill them
• water
• freezer space
• a piece of ground you are allowed to dig up

Method:

• Fill the milk cartons with sand

• Add water to thoroughly wet sand

• Freeze solid

• Meanwhile, dig a hole about a metre square.

• When the sand is completely frozen, tear off the cartons. Lay the two frozen bars in the excavated hole across one another. Cover them with the soil you have dug out.

• Leave the bars to thaw. Now you can begin to excavate your site. Moisten the ground you have dug up.
   Excavate carefully with a trowel, being careful not to disturb the layers as you unearth them.
   Draw on graph paper what you observe as you proceed.

From stains like these, the archaeologist can reconstruct what a three-dimensional feature must have looked like. If the discolourations had been traces of wood, they might represent part of a house foundation.

2. How important do you think it is to make a record at the end of each day? Would every second or third day do as well? Test your memory. Take turns with a friend.

• Have your friend put half a dozen small articles on a tray. You could use a key, button, piece of wood, eraser, spoon, a stone or bone.

• Look at the assortment very carefully for two minutes. Now you are the detective.

• Look away and write down what you saw. Draw each object in its position on the tray.

• Later, have your friend make another collection of small objects. Look at them carefully, as you did before. But this time wait for two hours before you write up your record.

Was your second record as complete as the first?

Louis Badone

Qaummaarviit

Baffin Island

Mipook was pleased to scc the white whalebone on the rocky beach. The huge arvik (or bowhead whale) that supplied the Thule people with vast quantities of food was here. The island would be a good place to settle. He ran to help pull up and unload the umiak, the large boat used for carrying women, children and supplies. He had his own sealskin kayak, the small, swift hunter's craft. Proudly, he fingered the piece of sinew around his neck. It had a knot for each one of his years—15 now.

Generations before, Mipook's ancestors had left their home in Alaska and moved steadily eastward. Tradition said that the earliest of them followed the bowhead whales. Perhaps they were also moving toward the source of metal traded from Greenland. About a thousand years ago they took advantage of a warming trend in the weather to expand their territory. Some of their ways had to change. In Alaska there was plenty of wood with which to build their houses, but here they had to

Robert McGhee

use rocks to form walls and whalebone for rafters and supports. Fortunately, the Thule people were the most inventive of Arctic explorers.

Now Mipook's group had reached an island called Quammaarviit, "the place that shines," near the present town of Iqaluit, on Frobisher Bay, Baffin Island. Around him Mipook saw traces of the Tunnit, an earlier people who had once lived on the island—rings of stones which had held their skin tents down and patches of greener vegetation where their refuse dumps had been. Theirs was a much harder life, he thought; they had no large sleds or boats to hunt from or carry meat. They had to keep moving to find food, mostly seals and other marine animals caught at the edge of sea ice.

He was glad that his people, the Thule, had better ways of hunting. With his bow and arrow he had already killed a large bull caribou and had used his bola to bring down birds.

"Arvik, arvik (whale, whale)!" shouted the women and children in the umiak. Mipook quickly hurled his harpoon and tossed the sealskin floats onto the water. The head of the harpoon detached as it sunk into the great whale's flesh. It turned sideways and hooked in as the line tightened. The floats would slow the animal down and mark the spot where it

Above: Two ground stone ulus are small replicas of the type used by the women to scrape skins for clothing.

Below is a Thule food cache. The ability to transport food by boat or sled back to store in caches allowed the Thule to settle in winter communities.

Louis Badone

lay. The whales could be 15 metres long and weigh many tonnes. There would be meat and blubber in the caches for a long time.

"Aya, aya, ya," the people chanted, "We shall not go hungry this winter!"

At Qaummaarviit over 3000 tools and 20 000 pieces of bone were excavated from five Thule winter houses by Douglas Stenton of the Canadian Circumpolar Institute (University of Alberta). This evidence of a rich lifestyle helps to explain why the approximately twenty-five people chose the island for their village. Apart from whale bone, remains of seal and caribou represented the highest percentage of finds. Bones of arctic hare, fox, walrus and polar bear were also found. The Thule people would have been attracted by this combination of abundant food from both the sea and the land.

Their advanced technology allowed them not only to procure meat and blubber but also to transport and store them for winter use in stone caches near their houses. In the long dark time they had the leisure to sing and tell stories around the light and warmth of seal oil lamps.

Weather in the Arctic makes working conditions different from other areas for the archaeologist. In comparison with southern Canada there are few settlements and these are far apart, some marked only by a ring of vegetation. The year-round frost line, below which the ground never thaws, lurks very close to the surface; usually permafrost is only a few centimetres away. Although this makes digging difficult, it also slows down the decay of bone, ivory and wood.

The people at Qaummaarviit were not alone, as Douglas Stenton found in his survey around nearby Peterhead Inlet. Sixteen Thule houses were uncovered in the area. He tells the story of one day's discoveries.

It was the end of a cold day in September, the end of the digging season, too. In fact, it was so cold that some of

the crew had made a snowman up on the ridge. We had been working in one part of House 11 all day scraping through 30 centimetres of gravel with no trace of an artifact or feature. Why did we keep going? It's hard to say, a hunch perhaps. But sometimes persevering pays off. Suddenly we saw the glint of yellowed ivory and some fragments of baleen (a type of whalebone). We rigged up a tarpaulin over the square and tried to thaw out the permafrost using a Coleman stove. Because the ground was so solidly frozen we made slow progress extracting what turned out to be an ivory ice pick. In the course of scratching around, right under the spot where the heel of a crew member had been, the tines of an ivory comb appeared. We thought at first they were just fragments. But we heated up a pail of water, got a small paint brush and carefully brushed the earth away bit by bit. It took about half an hour to clear it. Then it lifted right out beautifully.

This part of the house turned out to have many finds. It contained lots of knotted baleen, probably used as a drying rack; the ivory ice pick; part of an ivory sled runner; a piece of a soapstone pot; bits of whalebone and food debris; and a hank of human hair. The hair is interesting because few samples have been found. It will be analyzed in a lab to see what we can learn about the diet of the person who lived in the house. But the comb was really beautiful![6]

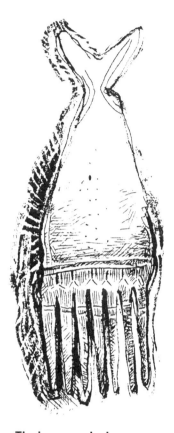

The ivory comb above was found beneath the boot of one of the crew. The parallel lines around the outside and the decoration are typical of early Thule sites in the eastern Arctic.

As in Fort Selkirk, local people are involved in examining their origins. Through courses offered at Arctic College in Iqaluit, many students, both Inuit and non-Inuit, learn about the ways in which cultures are studied, and have helped with the excavations. The elders have shared their knowledge of traditional ways. All the information obtained will be used in Baffin Island schools, often in the form of talks given by members of the archaeological team.

Clues

The archaeologist's field report of his or her season's work is the link between the excavated site and the public that makes use of the new knowledge.

The work in the field is only part of the archaeologist's job. At the end of the digging season, back in the office, he or she meets a new challenge. There are folders of daily record forms for each individual square, maps, drawings, photographs, and perhaps thousands of artifacts to organize, classify and interpret. How can all this be pulled together to make a comprehensive and intelligible picture?

Archaeologists realize that excavation of a site destroys it. Features cannot be dug twice. Only by careful and detailed reporting can the information gained be made available for future use.

First, the catalogued artifacts are classified into different types, perhaps according to form, as with the projectile points, perhaps by how they were used—as weapons, tools, or in cooking. Now the archaeologist can study a class of objects rather than so many individual items. Through the numbers given to each piece, and the careful recording of each day's work, the artifact can be related to the site. Where it was found and what it was found with are the essential clues to understanding what meaning and importance the piece had for the people who used it.

The written part of the report is made up of an introduction and history of the site, the purpose of the dig, the methods used and the results. Then the archaeologist must interpret the findings. What do they tell about the way the community lived? How did people deal with their environment? Were there any changes over time in the way they lived? For example, meetings with Inuit elders of the area helped to explain some of the ways artifacts and structures could have been used.

Douglas Stenton listed his findings in each structure on Qaummaarviit. Then the structures were considered together, to form a picture of life on the island. From there he surveyed around Peterhead Inlet and found that other Thule people had lived in the area. By enlarging the circle of investigation and comparing remains, archaeologists are able to trace the Thule back to their Alaskan homeland.

The evidence in Qaummaarviit Historic Park shows that they were among the most resourceful of pre-industrial people in coping with a challenging and unforgiving climate.

DOWN The Time Tunnel

Winter was the time for socializing in the comfortable Thule house. Sometimes two houses would be built joined to one another to make a place big enough for people to meet. They told stories, sang songs to the beat of a drum, and played games.

Two of their popular games follow. Make your own versions with modern materials.

1. About 25 small bones from a seal flipper are put into a sealskin mitt. A loop is made in a length of sinew. The loop is also put into the mitt and pushed to the bottom. Holding the open end of the mitt tight, shake up the bones. Put the mitt on a flat surface and slowly pull the sinew out. When you feel it catch on to some bones, pull it all the way.

The different shaped bones are given names—woman, man, musk-ox, sled, dog, girl, boy, etc. You might catch two girls and a dog, or a man and a musk-ox. Turns are taken until all the seal bones are out. The children who play this game then make up a story with their pieces and act it out.

The Inuit use a sealskin mitt and bones; you could use your own mitt with marked wooden pieces or chicken bones. You could give your pieces names from your world and make up your own unique stories.

mitten

sinew

Bones

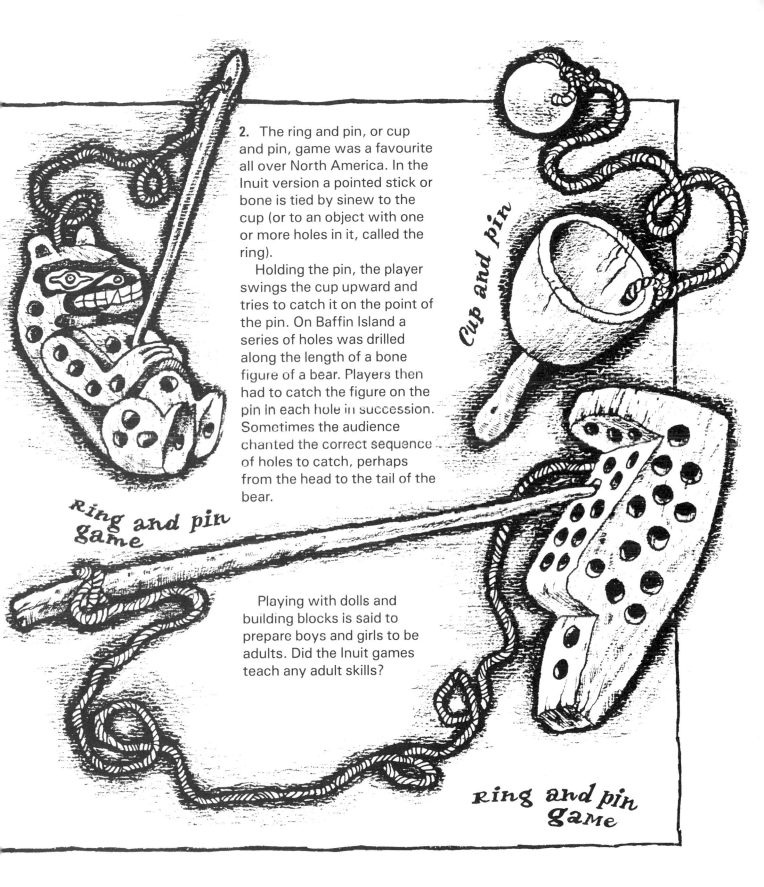

2. The ring and pin, or cup and pin, game was a favourite all over North America. In the Inuit version a pointed stick or bone is tied by sinew to the cup (or to an object with one or more holes in it, called the ring).

Holding the pin, the player swings the cup upward and tries to catch it on the point of the pin. On Baffin Island a series of holes was drilled along the length of a bone figure of a bear. Players then had to catch the figure on the pin in each hole in succession. Sometimes the audience chanted the correct sequence of holes to catch, perhaps from the head to the tail of the bear.

Playing with dolls and building blocks is said to prepare boys and girls to be adults. Did the Inuit games teach any adult skills?

Cup and pin

Ring and pin game

ring and pin game

The Globe and Mail,
July 30, 1991

For nearly a thousand years the bones lay undisturbed on the Arctic tundra, touched only by winds that blew through the rocks piled atop the ancient graves. Then from 1921 to 1924, without permission from Canada's Inuit, anthropologists opened those graves and took the skeletal remains for scientific study . . . Today many native leaders view most, if not all, of that scientific study as little more than a desecration of their ancestors.

Fortunately, archaeologists are now much more sensitive to the feelings of the descendants of those whose graves they uncover. On Qaummaarviit Douglas Stenton found ancient skeletons enclosed in stone cairns. Without disturbing them, he made careful notes of what he could see. The form of the burial could be compared with other known Thule sites. Objects which were to accompany the deceased to the other world were also observed. Some grave goods, like harpoon heads, would be useful in the next life.

Scientists have learned much about the pattern of people's lives from investigations of the dead.

Analysis of the frozen bodies of members of the ill-fated Franklin expedition in the Arctic showed that a possible cause of death was lead poisoning from tins containing their food.

However, any examination of burials should only be done with respect for both the living and the dead, and only with the permission of descendants, where that is possible. Archaeologists realize that these burials contain the remains of human beings who had feelings, wishes, dreams and aspirations, as we all have. If bones and grave goods are to be studied, they must later be buried or treated in the way that the deceased person might have wished.

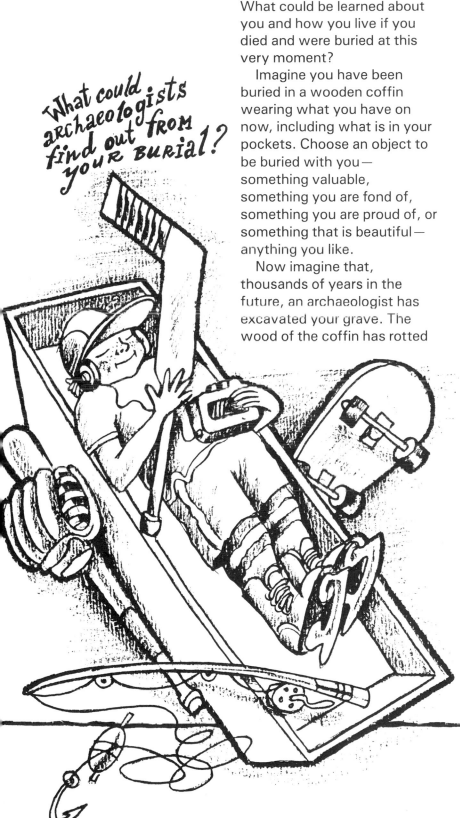

What could be learned about you and how you live if you died and were buried at this very moment?

Imagine you have been buried in a wooden coffin wearing what you have on now, including what is in your pockets. Choose an object to be buried with you—something valuable, something you are fond of, something you are proud of, or something that is beautiful—anything you like.

Now imagine that, thousands of years in the future, an archaeologist has excavated your grave. The wood of the coffin has rotted away, leaving only stains in the earth. All that is left of your body is your skeleton.

What would have happened to the other things—a watch, buttons, your shoes, a necklace?

What could archaeologists find out from your burial?

Would they be able to tell your name, whether you were a boy or a girl, or how old you were when you died?

Would they know if you were basically a healthy person, or whether you had had illnesses, trouble with your teeth, or been in an accident?

Could they tell if you were wealthy, or who your parents were?

Would they be able to form a picture of what you had looked like?

What could they find out about the way you had lived—whether you went to school or were a member of a religious group?

Finally, could they tell why, how and when you died? Would the archaeologist be able to form a picture of your culture, the way people like you live today?

Would the archaeologist be able to form a picture of your culture, the way people like you live today?

How Can I Dig into the Past?

Opportunities for Hands-on History

Archaeologists believe it is very important not to go out on your own to dig and collect artifacts. This is called "pot-hunting" and is considered selfish and outrageous since it destroys the record left in the ground by the features and artifacts.

Detectives need all the pieces of the puzzle to put the whole picture together. Every bit of clay sherd helps to put the pot together. An unthinking souvenir collector may casually pick up the very bit that has the meaningful decoration or shape.

Imagine the scene of a crime—the library of a mansion. The wall safe has been robbed. An observant reporter sees the glint of a small stone lying between cigarette butts in an ashtray. Being unscrupulous, and thinking the gem may be valuable, she or he quickly pockets ash tray and all.

Will this make it harder for the police to find the robber? Possibly. There may be fingerprints on the ashtray. The brand of the cigarettes may be distinctive. If there is more than one brand, there may have been more than one person involved. The small stone could be missing from a ring or brooch—whose? The evidence of small things helps police detectives and it helps archaeological detectives in the same way. Every scrap is valuable.

Well, then, do you have to be an archaeologist to work on a dig? Archaeologists must go to university for four or more years, and gain experience on other excavations, before they can be licensed to undertake one of their own.

However, there are lots of opportunities for people without special training to work or volunteer on a dig.

Many sites, like Head-Smashed-In Buffalo Jump in Alberta and Ste. Marie-among-the-Hurons in Ontario, have programmes for school groups.

Others encourage members of the public to join in. In downtown Winnipeg, the archaeology programme at the forks of the Red and Assiniboine Rivers uses volunteer diggers, laboratory helpers and computer assistants. The Barnum House in Ontario invited people to help them uncover the foundations of a woodshed and traces of an earlier house that had burned down in 1814.

Archaeological Resource Centre, Toronto Board of Education

Some school boards have classes in archaeology, and give high school history credits for the completion of an archaeological course. In Ontario the Archaeological Resource Centre of the Toronto Board of Education gives classes as well as allowing individual volunteers of all ages to take part in their excavations. The Boyd Archaeological Field School, north of Toronto, also offers a high school credit course.

To find out if there are projects like this in your area ask at your local museum, historical society, or First Nations cultural centre.

You can also contact your nearest university department of archaeology or anthropology for news of their excavations and requirements for volunteers.

A very good place to enquire is your provincial archaeological society. The Ontario Archaeological Society has a programme called Passport to the Past. If you are on their register you will receive bulletins about opportunities for volunteering in field activities, surveying or laboratory work. They also list training courses you can attend and trips to archaeological sites which are open to the public. The Saskatchewan Archaeological Society has a field school at Lake Diefenbaker which runs weekend summer courses. The whole family can enrol.

Volunteers have played a very important role in Canadian archaeology. Some of the most exciting discoveries have been made by people like you, working along with the professionals. And who knows what might lie in your backyard?

If you do find anything that you think might be an artifact, take it to your local university or archaeological society. Other places to contact are the Canadian Museum of Civilization in Ottawa or the Canadian Parks Service.

More sources of information:

Archaeological Society of Alberta
    2846--6a Avenue South, Lethbridge AB T1J 1H2
    (403) 329-6853
    Chapters: Calgary, Edmonton, Lethbridge, Underwater Society
    Publications: ALBERTA ARCHAEOLOGICAL REVIEW

Archaeological Society of British Columbia
    P.O. Box 520, Station A, Vancouver, BC V6C 2N3
    Membership Secretary (604) 736-4708
    Journal: THE MIDDEN

Manitoba Archaeological Society
    Box 1171, Winnipeg, MB R3C 2Y4
    Office and Reading Room: 438 Lombard Ave #167 (Grain Exchange Building), Winnipeg.
    Office Manager (204) 942-7243

Archaeological Services
    Provincial Parks and Historic Sites Branch
    P.O. Box 12345, Marysville Place, Fredericton NB E3B 5C3
    Archaeology Director (506) 453-2793

Newfoundland and Labrador Association of Amateur Archaeologists
    P.O. Box 8214, Station A, St. John's NF A1B 3N4

Archaeology Unit
    Prince of Wales Northern Heritage Centre
    Government of the Northwest Territories
    P.O. Box 130, Yellowknife, NWT X1A 2L9
    Administrator (403) 873-7686

Nova Scotia Archaeology Society
    c/o Nova Scotia Museum (902) 429-4610
    1747 Summer Street, Halifax, NS B3H 8A6
    Meetings are held fourth Tuesday each month September-April in the Auditorium of the Nova Scotia Museum.

The Ontario Archaeological Society
  126 Willowdale Ave., Willowdale, ON M2N 4Y2
  Administrator (416) 730-0797
  Chapters: Grand River Waterloo, London, Niagara, Ottawa,
Thunder Bay, Toronto, Windsor
  Publications: Journal: ONTARIO ARCHAEOLOGY
  Newsletter: ARCH NOTES

Prince Edward Island Museum & Heritage Foundation
  2 Kent Street, Charlottetown, NB C1A 1M6
  Executive Director (902) 892-9127

Ministère des Affaires Culturelles
  Service des Dosier du Patrimoine
  225 Grand-Allée est, Bloc C-2, rez-de-chaussée, Québec, PQ
G1R 5G5
  (418) 643-7658

Saskatchewan Archaeological Society
  816 1st Ave N., #5, Saskatoon, SK S7K 1Y3
  Executive Director (306) 664-4124
  Chapters: Bear Hills, Regina, South West, Vidora, West
Central
  Publications: SASKATCHEWAN ARCHAEOLOGY, SAS
NEWSLETTER

Heritage Branch
  Dept. Tourism, Heritage and Cultural Resources
  P.O. Box 2703, 211 Hawkins Street, Whitehorse, YK Y1A
2C6
  Director (403) 667-5386

Archaeological Survey of Canada,
  Canadian Museum of Civilization, Ottawa ON, K1A 0M8
(819) 997-8200

Parks Canada, Ottawa, ON, K1A 0H3 (613) 994-2595

Some Words to Know

archaeology the study of people through their physical remains, the things they used and left behind

artifact an object that has been altered or used by people

balk wall of an excavation square, often showing strata

base line the known east-west line used as a geometrical base for making other survey measurements

Borden number stands for the geographical location of a site in Canada

culture the learned behaviour of a group of people which is passed on to the next generation

datum a fixed point chosen to act as a reference for measurements when mapping a site. It is located at one corner of the grid

ethnology the study of groups of people or cultures

excavation systematic digging of an archaeological site

feature marks or remains in the earth that tell of people's activities. They cannot be easily moved.

grid a fixed pattern of horizontal and vertical lines laid out on a site to form units of equal size

midden the area where refuse is dumped

postmould a dark stain in the earth indicating the remains of a wooden post

relative dating comparing artifacts or features with others whose age is known

replication reproducing an artifact in the same way that it was made originally

report the archaeologist's account of everything he or she has found out in the dig

seriation a way of arranging artifacts by changes in style or composition in order to date them

sherd a broken piece of earthenware

site a place where there is evidence of human activity

society the way of life of a community

stratigraphy describes layers of deposits, or strata

stratum, strata a stratum is a layer of deposits in the earth. More than one are called strata, and differ in colour or texture

Use the extra space to add some more terms and definitions.

110

Footnotes:

(1) *The Vinland Sagas: the Norse Discovery of America*, trans. by Magnus Magnusson and Hermann Palsson. Penguin Books, Harmondsworth, 1965 p. 54

(2) Ingstad, Helge. *Westward to Vinland*. Macmillan, Toronto, 1969 p. 115

(3) Quoted in *Louisbourg, Key to a Continent* by F. Downey. Prentice-Hall, New Jersey, 1965 p. 5

(4) Quoted in Albert Almon, *Louisbourg—the Dream City* (Glace Bay, N.S. 1934) p. 80

(5) Moore, Christopher. "The Treasures of Louisbourg", in *Canadian Heritage*, Vol. 10, Issue 5

(6) Declaration of J.H. Henchey against William Tracey, July 1895, Court Document, Quebec

(7) Douglas Stenton, conversation with the author, August, 1991

Acknowledgements

Many time detectives, archaeologists, scientists and others, have been extremely helpful in providing information and illustrations. Without their expert knowledge this book would lack all the detail and substance which makes each of these sites so fascinating.

The author acknowledges with much gratitude her debt, first, to The Ontario Archaeological Society, especially Ellen Blaubergs and Charles Garrad; The Toronto Board of Education Archaeological Resource Centre (special thanks to Michelle Tremblay); and to the following individuals: Birgitta Wallace (L'Anse aux Meadows), Charles Burke and Heather Gillis (Louisbourg), Renée Côté and Louise Décarie (Place Royale), William Finlayson, Garry Hutton, Jock McAndrew (Crawford Lake), Larry Pavlish for help with dating in those two sites, Peter Priess and Linda Seyers (Lower Fort Garry), Jack Brink, Brian Kooyman, Brian Reeves, Christopher Williams (Head-Smashed-In-Buffalo Jump), Andrew Clifton, George MacDonald, Joanne MacDonald (Kitwanga), Jacques Cinq-Mars and Ruth Gotthardt (Bluefish Cave and Fort Selkirk), David Monteith and Douglas Stenton (Qaummaarviit), Robert McGhee for help with the last two sites.

Thank you all for your friendly cooperation and the pleasure which our association has given.

The author would also like to acknowledge the support and companionship of her husband, Louis Badone, whose technical expertise was often called upon.